Simple Sermons on

# new
# testament
# texts

# Simple Sermons on

# *new testament texts*

by
W. HERSCHEL FORD, B.A., D.D.

ZONDERVAN PUBLISHING HOUSE
OF THE ZONDERVAN CORPORATION
GRAND RAPIDS, MICHIGAN 49506

# Contents

# Contents

# Foreword

What! Another "Simple Sermon" book by that fellow Ford? Yes, here it is with ten more sermons. I hope they will help preachers and Christian workers and all who read them.

We are living in the Space Age when men circle the earth and walk on the moon. The experts tell us that before long men will be living on permanent platforms in outer space.

But wherever he is and whatever he is doing, man will still need God, the salvation He offers through the Lord Jesus Christ and the comforting and strengthening which the Holy Spirit can give him.

So I pray that these simple messages will lead men to Christ and to the more abundant life. As always, I say that preachers and Christian workers are free to use these sermons as their very own.

W. HERSCHEL FORD

*4719-D Skillman Street*
*Dallas, Texas 75206*

Simple Sermons on

# new
# testament
# texts

# 1.

# The Biography of a Christian

*Acts 11:26*

The word "Christian" is mentioned only three times in the Bible. In *Acts 28:28* we hear King Agrippa saying to Paul, "Almost thou persuadest me to be a Christian." In *1 Peter 4:16* we hear Peter saying, "If any man suffer as a Christian, let him not be ashamed, but let him glorify God on this behalf." Then we have our text which says that the "disciples were called Christians first in Antioch." So in this message I want us to think of the biography of a Christian.

I like to read the life-stories of great men. I like to read about the first man, made in the image of God. I like to read about Abraham, who was called "the friend of God." I like to read about Joseph, the best man in the Old Testament. I like to read about Moses, the greatest man in the Old Testament. I like to read about Daniel, the man of courage who slept with the lions. I like to read about David, the sweet singer of Israel, who was "a man after God's own heart."

Then I come to the New Testament and I like to read about John the Baptist, the mighty forerunner of Christ. I like to read about John, who gave us a view of heaven in the Revelation. I like to read about Simon Peter, who denied the Lord Jesus but who later won 3,000 people to Christ in one day. I like to read about Paul, who influenced the world more than any man this side of Jesus. And of course,

I like to read about the greatest life of all, that of the Lord Jesus Christ, God's only begotten Son.

But I come today to give you the biography of a Christian. Not some outstanding man of God, not some faithful missionary, not any particular Christian, but any Christian, great or small, rich or poor. Now what is a Christian? Dr. R. A. Torrey said that a Christian was (1) anyone who came to God as a lost sinner, (2) who repents of his sin and trusts Christ as his personal Saviour, (3) who surrenders to Him as Lord and Master, (4) who confesses Him as such before the world, and (5) who strives to please Him in everything from day to day. So let us examine his life story.

## I. The Birth of a Christian

His birth is different from every other birth, for other births are of the flesh while the Christian's birth is of the Spirit. Jesus told Nicodemus, the great religious leader, that he "must be born again." He would say the same thing to any lost person today. In fact, He said that unless a person is born again he would not "see the kingdom of God."

You may see the great redwood trees of California, but you'll never see the tree of life that grows in heaven unless you have been born again. You may see the cities of this world in all their splendor, but you'll never see the Holy City of the New Jerusalem unless you have been born again. You may see all of the countries of the world in all of their glory, but you'll never see the "land that is fairer than day" unless you have been born again. You may live in the finest house that money can buy, but you'll never see the Father's house of many mansions unless you've been born again. You may receive many degrees from the greatest colleges and universities of the world, but you'll never see heaven unless you have God's "B.A.," His "Born Again" degree.

Sometime ago a group of Christian young people took a

poll in a certain Ohio city. They asked 675 people the question, "How does a person get to heaven?" Eighty-five percent of this number could not give a Bible answer. Some said you could go to heaven by joining a church and attending its services. Some said you could get to heaven by living a good life. Some said you could get to heaven by reading the Bible. Some said that you could work your way to heaven. Some said that you would go to heaven if you were sincere in what you believed.

But the Bible says that we get to heaven by being born again, by being washed in the blood of Calvary's Lamb. A Christian is not born in the delivery room of baptism. He is not born in the maternity ward of church membership. He is not born in the hospital of good works. He is born at Calvary when he looks away from sin and self and looks up in faith to the Saviour, the Lord Jesus Christ.

Some years ago I knew a small boy who lived in a Southern town. His mother died when he was four, his father married again and both the father and stepmother were very strict with him. The family was terribly poor. This little boy hardly ever went to church, because the other members of the family did not attend. He was a poor, lost, lonely, little boy. Then two good men of God, a preacher and a singer, came to town to conduct a revival meeting. That little boy went to the services every night. He heard the preaching and the singing and he became convicted of his sin. He knew he was lost and he wanted to be saved. He sat there in the balcony every night and watched others go forward to trust Christ and be saved and he wanted to do the same thing. But someone had given him the erroneous idea that if anyone joined the church they would have to give a certain amount each month and he knew his family could not afford that. So every night he went home past the cemetery where his mother was buried, went to bed and wept himself to sleep.

Then some years later he went to the big city to make his living. About that time Billy Sunday came to that city for one of his campaigns. That boy went to the meeting several nights. Then on a Sunday afternoon Billy Sunday preached to men and boys only and that boy was present. When the great evangelist gave the invitation for men and boys to come forward and accept Christ (he called it "hitting the sawdust trail") that boy went forward and gave his heart to Jesus Christ. After that even all of life changed for that boy. He was never to be the same again. I know this is a true story because I was that boy. I don't know what the great evangelist preached about that day, I don't know what song Homer Rodeheaver sang, I only know that on that afternoon, the best I knew how, I trusted Christ as my Lord and Saviour and that He saved me that day through His wonderful grace.

> I had walked life's way with an easy tread,
> Had followed where comforts and pleasures led,
> Until one day in a quiet place,
> I met my Master face to face.
>
> With station and rank and wealth for a goal,
> Much thought for the body, but none for the soul,
> I had entered to win in life's mad race,
> When I met my Master face to face.
>
> I had built my castles and reared them high,
> Till their towers pierced the blue of the sky.
> I had sworn to rule with an iron mace,
> When I met my Master face to face.
>
> I met Him and knew Him and blushed to see,
> That His eyes, filled with sorrow, were fixed on me.
> And I faltered and fell at His feet that day,
> While my castles melted and vanished away.

Melted and vanished and in their place,
Naught else could I see but the Master's face,
And I cried aloud, "Oh make me meet
To follow the steps of Thy wounded feet."

My thought is now for the souls of men,
I have lost my life to find it again,
E'er since one day in a quiet place,
I met my Master face to face.

## II. The Life of a Christian

1. *It is a life of communication.* That is a big word to-day. Lack of communication in the family causes trouble, and when we who are in the family of God don't communicate with Him we are in trouble. The Christian has an open line of communication with God. When we open the Bible God speaks to us, when we go upon our knees in prayer we speak to God. It is a sad day in a Christian's life when he cuts this line of communication.

Dr. Carter Helm Jones was pastor of a church in Philadelphia. He lived in a large two-story house. But on the third story there was a lone room which he called the "Sky Room." In this room he had a chair, a table and a Bible, and he went up to that room when he wanted to be alone with God. One day he came in all out of sorts, after a long season of visits and conferences. He told his wife he was going up to the "Sky Room." She was always glad to see him go up there for he always came back in a better humor. After he had gone into the room he heard the patter of little feet on the steps, followed by a timid knock on the door. When he opened the door there was his little four-year-old daughter looking up at him. In a very angry voice he said, "Now what do you want?" And the little one said, "Nothing, daddy, except that I wanted to love you a little bit. You've been so busy lately we haven't had any loving."

Then he knelt down, the little girl hugged him and kissed him and then scampered on down the steps. Dr. Jones said that he went over to the chair, fell upon his knees and said, "Dear God, that's what I need. I've been so busy lately that I haven't had time to love You. And now I come to tell You that I love You and appreciate all you've done for me."

That's what we need, also. We must never get too busy to communicate with the Heavenly Father. Jesus kept that line always open, He was always in close touch with God.

2. *It is a life of compassion.* Once upon a time there was an Oriental king who would dress himself in a resplendent uniform, put on all of his medals and strut up and down before a large mirror. He thought only of himself while his people suffered and starved. But one of his elder statesmen felt there was some good in the king, if he could only be brought to get his mind off himself and think of his people. So one night the older man had the large mirror torn out and a window put in its place. The next morning when the king came to admire himself he saw not his own reflection in the mirror, but he saw his people in all of their need.

He saw a weary mother and her children, he saw tired men bent beneath heavy burdens, he saw hungry children foraging in the garbage cans for food. Moved with compassion he took off his resplendent uniform, donned some simple clothes and went out among his subjects. He soon learned their needs and set about to relieve their suffering. And in this way he found true happiness.

Yes, Jesus would say, "If you want to find happiness and satisfaction you must look away from yourself and look at those who are lost and lonely and needy. You must give your life away in the service of God and man."

3. *It is a life of a forgiving spirit.* There are those who are going to hurt us even as we often hurt them. But as

Christians we are not to hold grudges, for these become heavy weights to pull us down and away from God. The Bible tells us that if we don't forgive others we need not expect God to forgive us. If we are to be like Him we must have a forgiving spirit.

Some years ago I held a revival in Muskogee, Oklahoma. One day I went out to an Indian church and I read there the inscription on a stone which portrayed one of the finest examples of forgiveness I have ever seen. Let me read you that inscription:

> We have been broken up and moved six times. We have been despoiled of our property. We thought that when we moved across the Missouri River and had paid for our homes in Kansas we were safe, but in a few years the white men wanted our country. We had good farms, built comfortable houses and big barns. We had schools for our children and churches where we listened to the same gospel the white man listened to. The white man came into our country from Missouri and drove our cattle and horses away and if our people followed them, they were killed.
>
> We try to forget these things, but we would not forget that the white man brought us the blessed gospel of Christ, the Christian's hope. This more than pays for all we have suffered. We forgive everything else.
>
> — Charles Journeycake
> Chief of the Delawares  April 1886

This should be our spirit, the spirit of love which made Christ say on the cross, "Father, forgive them, for they know not what they do." If He could forgive those who were putting Him to death surely we ought to forgive those who mistreat us.

4. *It is sometimes a life of sin.* Yes, all of us have sinned and come short of the glory of God. "If we say that we have no sin, we deceive ourselves, and the truth is not in us" (1 John 1:8). But there is a blessed relief for us in the very

next verse, "If we confess our sins, he is faithful and just to forgive us our sins, and to cleanse us from all unrighteousness" (1 John 1:9). It is sweet to know that when we come in confession and repentance to Him He will wash all our sin away.

5. *It is a life of service.* How can we serve the Lord? We can serve Him by consecrated Christian living. We can serve Him by giving Him some of our time. We can serve Him by using our talents for Him. We can serve Him by giving Him our tithes and offerings. We can serve Him by telling others of His saving grace. We can serve Him by our faithfulness to His church.

6. *It is a life of witnessing and winning.* Some years ago I conducted a revival in a church in Louisiana. One night the pastor pointed out a man to me and said, "He is one of my most faithful deacons. His wife sings in the choir and is superintendent of the Junior Department of our Sunday school. They are the finest couple in our church." On Friday of that week this couple invited the pastor and singer and me to their home for a meal. A fine woman had prepared the meal and now served it in a most gracious manner. After the meal I wanted to go back into the kitchen and thank this fine servant for her good service. I asked the hostess what church her cook attended and she said, "I do not know." Now remember that this lady sang in the choir, headed the Junior Department of the Sunday school and was active in every phase of the church life.

So I asked her another question, "Is your cook a Christian?" She bowed her head and said, "I don't know, I have never asked her." Then I asked her how long her cook had worked for her and she said, "Over three months." Now think of it, this woman was faithful and active in her church, but she had never been concerned about her servant's spiritual welfare, although they had been together every day for over three months. I went back in the kitchen and asked the cook if she knew the Lord Jesus as her Saviour and she replied, smilingly, "Yes sir, and I'se a member of the Jerusalem Baptist Church." But the faithful church member for whom she worked had never been concerned about her relationship to Christ.

There are those all around us who know not the Saviour. They are bound for an endless eternity. We are pretty poor Christians when we fail to witness to them about our wonderful Saviour.

7. *It is a life of love.* If we love Jesus we will love others, even though we often think that they are most unlovely. Jesus said, "By this shall all men know that ye are my disciples, if ye have love one to another" (John 13:35).

The beloved Apostle John served for many years as pastor of the church in Ephesus. Then he was banished to Patmos for his crime of preaching the Gospel. On the last day of his pastorate in Ephesus he was so feeble he had to be assisted to the pulpit by two of the deacons. Then one of the deacons said to him, "Pastor, this is probably the last time we'll ever be together. Do you have some special word for us, some advice that you think we need?" And he answered, "Little children, love one another." Then someone said, "What else, pastor?" And again the dear old preacher said, "Little children, love one another." Then someone said, "Surely, pastor, you want to tell us something else." And John answered, "That is enough."

And, my dear friends, it is enough. If all of us could just love one another in the right Christian way, our problems would be solved.

## III. THE DEATH OF A CHRISTIAN

Why, the Christian never really dies. His old body here gives out and is placed in the grave, but his spirit, his real self, lives on forever and ever. Yes, if the Lord tarries we will experience physical death, but we will still be alive in the grandest sense of the word.

Job asked the question, "If a man die, shall he live again?" And Jesus answered that question for us for all time. He died upon a Roman cross, He was buried in a borrowed tomb. But He burst the bonds of death and the grave and rose again. He lives, thank God, He lives. And He said in John 14:19, "Because I live, ye shall live, also."

The Bible has some wonderful things to say about the death of a Christian. Let us look at some of them, "Absent from the body, present with the Lord" (1 Cor. 5:8). "He giveth his beloved sleep" (Ps. 127:2). "Precious in the sight of the Lord is the death of his saints" (Ps. 116:15). "Blessed are the dead which die in the Lord from henceforth; Yea, saith the Spirit, that they may rest from their labors; and their works do follow them" (Rev. 14:13). "For me to live is Christ, and to die is gain" (Phil. 1:21).

Some time ago I visited my mother's grave in a cemetery in a little town in Georgia. Her body has lain in that grave for many years. If I could go into that grave I would see only the dust left there and I might say, "Is this all? Is this all that is left of my sweet mother?" Then from beyond the grave I would hear a voice saying, "This mortal must put on immortality and this corruption must put on incorruption." Then I would know for sure that my mother lives on. And because of Christ, every believer will live forever with Him.

## IV. The Future Life of a Christian

The Christian's future is as bright as the sunlight, as bright as the promise of God. God has prepared something wonderful for His children, He has prepared a glorious heaven for all His people. There is an old, old song which says, "This world is not my home, I'm just a-passing through." What is the song saying? Simply that God has a better life awaiting us, a life where sickness and sorrow and death can never touch us.

When I served as pastor of the First Baptist Church in El Paso, Texas, there lived in the city a wealthy man by the name of Lee Moor. His wife was a devoted Christian, but Mr. Moor was unsaved. Often I would visit in the home to take Mrs. Moor some of my books, and before I left we would always have prayer for Mr. Moor's salvation. Then, when I was in a revival in Roswell, New Mexico, Mrs. Moor died. Mr. Moor called me and asked me to come home and conduct her funeral. He told me he would supply a private plane for my trip, so I would not miss any services of the revival.

I flew back to El Paso and conducted the funeral service. Mr. Moor was really broken-hearted over the death of his wife. Mr. Clair Zachary of Dallas, president of the Southern Union Gas Company, flew out for the funeral and I had the pleasure of meeting him. Mr. Moor was a heavy stockholder in the Union Gas Company. After the funeral Mr. Zachary told me to come in to see him the next time I came to Dallas, where he was an active deacon in the First Baptist Church. So, the next time I was in Dallas I went to see him. We talked about Mr. Moor, who was then 83 years of age, and how we wanted to see him become a Christian. Before I left his office Mr. Zachary shut the door and that consecrated deacon and I knelt down and prayed for Mr. Moor.

I visited Mr. Moor on several occasions and often found him reading his New Testament which a friend, Frank Stewart, had given him. I explained God's plan of salvation and prayed with Mr. Moor on each visit. Then one Sunday morning when I gave the invitation he walked down the aisle and confessed his faith in Jesus Christ. I baptized him that night and he became a faithful Christian and church member. Three years later he died and I conducted his funeral. Mr. Zachary came out from Dallas and said to me, "It's altogether different this time, isn't it?" And it was, Jesus had made the difference and we felt then that Mr. Moor was "safe in the arms of Jesus." He left several million dollars to be used in building a home for homeless children and the Lee Moor Children's Home is now performing a great service to hundreds of needy children. Yes, as I think of Mr. Moor I remember that Christ makes the difference at the end of life's journey.

So let me ask you, "Have you had this wonderful new birth? Are you living at your best for Jesus? Are you ready for the great adventure called death? Are you laying up treasures in heaven that will bless you throughout eternity?"

John Wesley tells of a dream that he had. He dreamed he went down into hell and there he saw a great multitude of lost sinners. He asked someone there, "Are there any Methodists here?" And the answer was, "Yes." Then he asked, "Are there any Baptists here, any Catholics, any Presbyterians, any Lutherans, any Church of Christ members?" And the answer was always, "Yes." Then he said he awakened from his dream and was downcast because of what he had seen and heard. Then he slept again and dreamed that he had gone up into heaven, where he saw multitudes of people living in joy and happiness. He asked an angel the same question he had asked in hell, "Are there any Methodists here?" And the answer came back, "No." Then he asked, "Are there any Baptists here, any Presbyterians, any Catholics, any Lutherans, any members of the Church of Christ?" And the answer came back, "No."

Then he asked, "Who are these happy people, this great multitude?" And the answer came back, "These are simply those who have been redeemed by the blood of the Lamb."

Thank God, because of Jesus Christ, you and I, too, can be in that blood-washed throng, enjoying the eternal bliss which is waiting for all who are followers of our great Saviour.

# 2.

# God's Greatest Text for Christians

*Matthew 6:33*

Some years ago Duke University and the University of Tennessee were engaged in a crucial football game. With only a few seconds left to play Duke was leading Tennessee by a score of 13 to 9. Duke punted (kicked) the ball to Tennessee. A young man by the name of Red Harp caught the ball and began running down the field with it. His teammates gave him good blocking, he ran with all the speed he could command and soon ran across the goal line, made a touchdown and won the game. The crowds went wild. Later this fine athlete said, "I had been waiting all afternoon for that chance." When he started running down the field he had only one thing in mind and that was to cross the goal line. He put that first, nothing turned him to the right nor to the left.

That's the way God wants Christians to live. Jesus said that the kingdom of God, the cause of Christ, must be first in our lives. Nothing is to turn us to the right or to the left. We are to press forward for God, and as we go forward He will always supply our needs.

If a man makes a success of anything, he must put that thing first. Bobby Jones, Arnold Palmer, Jack Nicklaus and others have been champion golfers because they put golf first. Babe Ruth set a record of 714 home runs in his baseball career because he put that first. In 1927 Charles Lindbergh made the first solo flight across the Atlantic because he concentrated on that one thing. Thomas Edison perfected hundreds of inventions because he stayed in his laboratory long hours every day, putting all of his genius and efforts into this work. Spurgeon, Moody, Truett, Lee and others moved men toward God because preaching the Gospel was the paramount thing in their lives.

To be the Christian you ought to be and that God would have you to be, Jesus said, "Seek ye first the kingdom of God and His righteousness." Then He adds a gracious promise, "All these things shall be added unto you."

### I. Many People Put Other Things First

1. *Some people put business first.* I believe a man ought to work hard, he ought to give his best to his job, he ought to try to succeed, but his business interests should not come first. Here is a man who has a small job, he puts that job before everything else, he goes up and up until he reaches the top. The world says, "He is a wonderful success." But if he has left Christ out of his life, God says, "Thou fool, thou art a failure."

A certain railroad man lay dying. He had built a great railroad empire employing thousands of men; he had made millions of dollars. He reached up and grasped his son's hand and said, "Son, you are holding the hand of the world's greatest failure." "No," said the son, "you are not a failure, you have built a great railroad empire, you have employed thousands of men, you have made millions of dollars, you are certainly not a failure." "But," said the man, "in doing all this I have left Christ out and any man who does that is a failure." And he was right.

2. *Some people put the accumulation of wealth first.* The poet well said, "The world is too much with us." Men spend their time and energies gaining and getting, but they often

lose the sense of God. Another poet said, "I'm farther off from heaven than when I was a boy." That is true of many people. The more we seek for earthly things, the less of heaven we see.

Jenny Lind, the great singer, rose to the heights. She became very popular, earning great sums of money. But at the height of her glory she gave it all up. One day as she sat reading her Bible, someone asked her why she gave up the stage when she was at the very peak of success. Pointing to the sunset, she said, "My success made me think less of that," and laying her hand on her Bible, she said, "and it made me think little or nothing of this Book."

Yes, men can go on thinking of only material things until these things master them and cause them to forget God.

3. *Some people put ease and convenience first.* They want to lie in bed and sleep on Sunday morning instead of going to His house to worship Him. Then on Sunday night they say, "My home is so cozy, there are some good programs on television, I'll stay at home and take it easy." True, it is harder to go to church and serve God than to be at ease in Zion, but the Christian is not to take the easy way. His Saviour didn't.

4. *Some people put pleasure first.* Surely God is not opposed to your having a good time and enjoying life, but pleasure should not be the chief aim of life. Speaking to me of her pursuit of pleasure and her social activities, a young woman said, "This is my very life."

There are so many people today who get into the swim of pleasure so deeply that they forget the Lord God, they desecrate His day, they turn away from all the higher things of life.

5. *Some people put worldly organizations first.* Some years ago I talked to an older man about his relationship to Christ. He pointed to the lodge emblem in his lapel and

said, "This is my religion." But that religion will not stand the fires of God's judgment.

6. *Some people put their political party first.* Some men seem to be more concerned with electing the man of their party than with their own salvation. No matter who the candidate is, these men put their party first. But there ought to be principles in politics. You should vote for the man who is best qualified for the position.

7. *Some people put their country first.* Now it is fine to be patriotic, a man should love his country and be willing to serve it.

> "Breathes there a man with soul so dead,
> Who never to himself has said,
> 'This is my own, my native land'?"

Stephen Decatur said, "My country, may she always be right, but right or wrong, my country." That is a fine sentiment, but there is a loyalty higher than loyalty to one's country. It is one's loyalty to Christ. He should always come first.

### II.  WHAT IT MEANS TO SEEK THE KINGDOM OF GOD

First, we need to be sure that we are in His kingdom. One becomes a citizen of an earthly kingdom when he is born into it. And one becomes a citizen of God's kingdom when he is born into it through the new birth, the second birth. Jesus said to Nicodemus, "Except a man be born again, he cannot see the kingdom of God."

Not all people enter the kingdom under the same circumstances, although we must enter it by the same door of the new birth. Christ is the Christ of infinite variety. He healed many people while on the earth, but all under different circumstances. We have heard of men who stood up in some service and said, "On this very spot at such-and-such a time I was converted." But other Christians are not able to point to such a definite time and place.

A certain preacher tells about two colts he "broke in" when he was a boy. He said that he just went up to the first one, put the saddle on him and rode away. There was no rebelling, no opposition, no trouble. But the other colt was wild and obstreperous. Three men tried to ride him and he bucked and kicked until he threw each one to the ground. Finally, after much beating, and coaxing the colt gave up. "Now," said the preacher, "suppose those colts could talk and someone asked them when they were broken in. The first one would say, 'I don't know the exact minute, it just came natural, I guess.' But the second one would say, 'Oh, I'll never forget that day. They beat me and I fought back, I threw three men to the ground. But finally I gave in and there was no trouble after that.'"

It is the same way with conversion. One Christian will say, "I don't remember the exact minute. It seems that Christ just came quietly into my heart and I became His child." But another Christian would say, "I remember the very hour. I had fought the conviction of the Holy Spirit for weeks and God had to throw me down to the ground before I surrendered to Him."

We are told that in the South Sea Islands there is a flower which opens like the report of a gun. But the rose opens as quietly as the dawn. There is a difference in the way persons are converted, but the method doesn't matter. The main thing is that they can say, "Blessed assurance, Jesus is mine."

1. *To put God first means to conform one's life to His principles.* "Be not conformed to this world," says Paul. We are not to be like the world, but like Jesus. I carry a wallet in my hip pocket. In time it becomes conformed to the

curvature of my body, because it is so close to my body. Sometimes we are so close to the world we become like the world, but if we stay close to Christ we become like Him.

Martin Luther said, "When anyone knocks at the door of my heart and asks who lives there I say, 'Martin Luther used to live there, but he moved out and Jesus moved in.'"

Years ago in Atlanta I knew a dedicated deacon named I. B. Smith. He served as president of his railroad union. One night an official from the union's national headquarters attended a meeting where Mr. Smith presided. Later this official said to one of the union members, "This was a strange meeting, I never heard one curse word." And the man replied, "That was because I. B. Smith is our president." He was conforming his life to Christ and this was the secret of his influence.

I read of a man who had a strange malady. For some unknown reason, his body was shrinking. His weight had gone down to 97 pounds and his height was reduced 17 inches in ten years. God help us, some of us are shrinking spiritually, simply because we are not living up to Christ's principles for our lives.

2. *To put God first means to serve in His kingdom.* The Bible tells us that we are ambassadors for Christ. An ambassador is supposed to serve his king. When he was just a boy John Wanamaker began to put Christ first. In time he became a great business man. He had several stores, he made millions of dollars, he served as Postmaster General of the United States. But he always had time for the service of the Lord. In fact, he gave more time to the Lord's service than to his extensive business interests. He gave his money generously, he taught a large Bible class, he went to many places speaking for Christ. He visited the poor and he tried to win lost men to Christ. Wouldn't it be wonderful if every Christian business man served Christ in this manner?

3. *To put God first means to put His church first.* The church is the world's only divine institution, it is the only organization Christ left down here to do His work. The best way for us to serve Christ is through His church. What do we owe the local church?

(1) *We owe the church our presence.* Oliver Wendell Holmes said, "I have a little plant in my heart called reverence and it must be watered once a week." And that watering comes largely in the services of His church. As the automobile battery needs re-charging, as the watch needs winding, so do we need the strength that comes from our worship and fellowship in God's house.

A Christian never gets along well in his spiritual life if he is not faithful to his church. I have seen those who have been faithful begin to absent themselves from the church and I have seen them slip away into a worldly, practically useless life, and often into sin. Don't let it happen to you. You owe the church your presence.

(2) *We owe the church our prayers.* I have often wondered what mighty things a church could do if all the members of that church were fervent, praying Christians. Oh, what preaching, what singing, what soul-winning, what fellowship such a church would have.

(3) *We owe the church our payments.* In Guinness' *Book of World Records* I read that on a January day in 1916 the temperature in Browning, Montana, dropped from 44 degrees above to 56 degrees below in a few hours time — a drop of 100 degrees. And I have known people whose enthusiasm for their religion dropped just as fast and just as far when the preacher mentioned giving. Someone has said that "costless chatter" is easier than "digging up the dough."

Often we see a family budget written up by the experts in some national magazine. Usually a small amount for the church is listed at the end. But God's name should be always at the top and the amount should always be what the Bible teaches it should be — at least a tithe.

I read that one of John D. Rockefeller's daughters had a rope of emeralds that cost four million dollars. She wore these precious jewels just a few times before her death in 1932. Suppose this money had been used for the Lord. Think of the good it would have done, the souls it might have won, the churches that might have been built, the people who could have been helped by it.

The only money we save is what we give, the only treasure we lay up in heaven is what we send on ahead. We owe the church our payments.

(4) *We owe the church our power.* By this I mean that we owe her our talents, our time, our personalities, our service. It is simply not right for a Christian to give all of himself to the world and little or nothing to God and His church.

4. *To put God first means making Christ known to the world.* Today many people are prominent in the news of the world. The names of presidents and world rulers and actors and sports figures and entertainers are well-known to millions. But down in some dark place of the earth there is a little missionary couple working hard for the Lord. They have made many sacrifices for His sake, they have left their loved ones and friends thousands of miles behind, they have given up many of the so-called good things they had back home. But year by year they are winning a few souls to Christ, they are teaching them how to live and preparing them to die.

The world knows nothing about them, the world cares nothing about them. But when all the things of this world come to an end that little couple will be shining as the stars forever and ever, while the great and mighty figures of our times will be forgotten.

### III. God's Reward for Putting Him First

God puts it down very simply. "All these things shall be added unto you." What things? Jesus had been talking about material things, so He means that if we put Him first, He will give us all we need.

Why can't people see this? Why can't they see that God will keep His promise? Why can't they see that if they live for Christ and put Him first they'll never lack any needed thing? The psalmist knew this was true. He said, "I have been young, and now am old, yet have I not seen the righteous forsaken, nor his seed begging bread" (Ps. 37:25).

I have had many people come to the church begging for help, but upon questioning them I never found one who was really living for God. During the depression I knew many who lost their jobs but there was never a consecrated Christian in that group. God is faithful, He keeps His promises. Put Him first and then just watch Him bless you.

God's promise here is all-inclusive. He says that "all of these things" will be ours. There is a story in *The Arabian Nights* which tells of someone bringing a strange gift to the king. It was nothing but a nutshell. One of his men told the king to open the shell. He did so and behold, there proved to be a small tent within the shell. This tent immediately began to spread until it covered the king and his court and all of his army. That's the way it is with this promise Jesus made. It covers every need. So I appeal to you to give Him your best and He'll give His best back to you.

The Taj Mahal in India is said to be the most beautiful building in the world. There is a story behind it. A ruler loved his wife with a great love. Eight times she went down into the valley of death giving birth to a child. On the eighth journey she did not return. Her body was brought to a beautiful garden for burial. But her husband sat down beside the casket and wept. "Oh, my darling," he said, "you will have the beautiful palace I promised you, even though it will be your tomb." He employed 22,000 men to erect the building, the construction time was twenty years and the building cost twenty million dollars. Engraved on the building are these words, "To the memory of an undying love."

But I know of a greater love than that, the love of One who died on Calvary's cross for you and me. Christ gave His best for us. He calls upon us to give our best to Him. So I beseech you, by all that is noblest in life, by all that is divinest in faith, by all that is sweetest in your hope for eternity — give Him first place in your life and heart as a token of your undying love for Him. Yes, give Him your best and the best will come back to you.

# 3.

# From Here to Eternity

## 2 Timothy 1:12

When I want advice on some important matter I go to a person who knows about that matter. When I want medical advice I go to a reputable doctor. When I want legal advice I go to a good lawyer. When I want spiritual advice I go to a trustworthy preacher. But the best advice for us is found in the Word of God. And one of the best men to give spiritual advice is the Apostle Paul. Often we hear him saying, in the power of the Holy Spirit, "I know." With him it was not "I think" or "maybe," it was "I know."

In our text he tells us he knows certain things. He says, "I know whom I have believed, and am persuaded that he is able to keep that which I have committed unto him." He knows he has been saved because of his faith in Christ. He knows his soul is safe for heaven. He knows he will be rewarded for all he has done for Christ.

So as we speak on the subject, "From Here to Eternity," we look at four things.

(1) THE ATONEMENT THROUGH THE BLOOD
(2) THE ASSURANCE OF OUR SALVATION
(3) THE ACTIVITIES OF A CHRISTIAN
(4) THE ATTAINMENT AT THE END OF THE WAY

### I. THE ATONEMENT THROUGH THE BLOOD

Someone has pronounced this word as at-one-ment. In our natural state we are not at-one with God. We are separated from Him. How then can we get to be at-one with

God? There is only one way and that is through the atoning blood, through faith in the One who shed His blood for you on Calvary's cross. Jesus said, "No man cometh unto the Father, but by me" (John 14:6). He is the door, He is the way to God. There is no other way. Not by a good life, not by good works, not by baptism, not by church membership, but by Christ.

We must come as sinners, repenting of our sin and trusting Christ as our Saviour. One day I heard a man say, "I have never apologized to anyone in my life." I felt sorry for that man. He had never seen that he had ever done anything to hurt anyone else. But there is a greater tragedy and that is for a man never to feel he needs to come out of sin, weep over it, repent of it and come to Christ for forgiveness.

Jesus tells us about two men who went to church one day. The first man went right down to the front where everyone could see him and hear him. He prayed with himself, "God, I thank thee that I am not like some of the evil men in this community." Then he looked back toward the rear of the church and prayed, "I thank thee that I am not like this publican."

But the other man didn't go up to the front of the church. He stood way back, smote himself upon his breast, and prayed, "God be merciful to me, a sinner." That is the prayer the lost man must pray if he is to be saved. And I believe that is the prayer a saved man needs to pray every day, for the best of us are sinners. There are two kinds of sinners, the lost sinner and the saved sinner. And both need to repent of their sin.

An old man lay dying in one of our hospitals. In his last days he lost his eyesight so each day his granddaughter would come and read the Bible to him. One day she was reading 1 John and came to the verse which says, "If we confess our sins, he is faithful and just to forgive us our sins, and to cleanse us from all unrighteousness" (1 John 1:9).

The man said quickly, "Wait a minute, read that verse again." When the girl read the verse again the man said, "Does it really say that? Read it again." Then she read the verse again and he said, "Honey, put my fingers on what it says about the blood." Gently she took the old gnarled fingers and placed them on that passage. As his lips moved silently he repeated the words and God touched his soul. Just before he died he said, "You can say that I died believing in the blood of the Lord Jesus Christ." Of course, we know that the blood here simply means the death of Christ to save us from our sin. Oh, how we wish that everyone on earth would claim this promise. Our at-one-ment with God must come through the precious blood of Christ.

Why do men miss heaven and go to hell? The answer can be summed up in one word. Not because of adultery, not because of murder, not because of theft, not because of drunkenness. Men are lost because of neglect. The opportunity to turn away from sin to Christ is always there but men neglect to take advantage of the opportunity and thus they are forever lost.

## II. The Assurance of Our Salvation

We often wonder if we have been really and truly saved. Sometimes we feel that we have been, sometimes we are filled with doubts. Well, where can we get the answer? If we want the true answer it must come from the Bible. If we have come to God the Bible way, if we have carried out the Bible's directions, we can know that we are on the road to glory.

Listen to the most familiar verse in the Word of God. "For God so loved the world, that he gave his only begotten Son, that whosoever believeth in him should not perish, but have everlasting life" (John 3:16). If you have believed in Jesus Christ, if you have trusted in Him, the life He gives you is "everlasting." And how long is "everlasting"? It is forever. You have a life that never ends if you believe in Christ.

Listen to John 3:18, "He that believeth on him is not condemned: but he that believeth not is condemned already, because he hath not believed in the name of the only begotten Son of God." You see here that condemnation awaits the unbeliever but for the believer there is no condemnation.

Listen to *John 10:28-29* — "And I give unto them eternal life; and they shall never perish, neither shall any man pluck them out of my hand. My Father, which gave them me, is greater than all; and no man is able to pluck them out of my Father's hand." What is Jesus saying here? He is saying that both His hand and the Father's hand are around the believer and no force on earth or in heaven or hell can pluck him out of these hands.

Some people believe that a person may be saved today and lost tomorrow because of some sin he commits. They are saying that salvation is based on a man's perfection and we know that isn't true. We are not saved by living a perfect life for no man is perfect. If you say God can save you today with His marvelous salvation and the devil can snatch you away from God tomorrow, you are saying Satan is stronger than God. God has gone to great lengths to save us, He gave up His only begotten Son for our redemption. Do you think He will let one of His children go to hell after all He has done to save him?

"But," you say, "I may fall into sin, I may step aside." David did that. He sinned far more deeply than you will ever sin but God forgave him. He did not cast him aside. God called him "a man after my own heart."

A woman I know lived with her husband and two children in a small town in the south. He was very impractical and visionary, he was always going to make a million dollars. There came a time when he needed some money for one of his wild dreams so he stole it from the company he worked for. When the loss was discovered he was discharged. To keep him from going to prison the members of the family paid off the debt. He secured another job but his wife's heart was almost broken because of what he had done. Twenty-five years later she said to me, "In all of these years I have not mentioned that matter to him one time." What a fine spirit she had. And this is the way God treats us. When we come to Him through Christ, repenting of our sin and trusting His Son, He forgives and forgets.

Now I am sure that over the years this woman remembered her husband's mistake and was greatly hurt as she did remember. But in all those years until he died she never mentioned it. But God is greater than that. He said He would not only forgive our sins, but He would forget them. So when we face Him one day we will not be ashamed to stand before Him. He will have forgotten all our sins.

I remember a little chorus that expresses this truth:

> When God forgives He forgets,
> When God forgives He forgets,
> No longer He remembers our sins,
> When God forgives He forgets.

Some years ago a great European theologian and scholar came to America. He was a brilliant man who held many academic degrees and honors. He spoke in many churches and universities. One day at the close of one of his addresses, he opened up the meeting for questions. A man in the back of the room stood up and said, "Doctor, with all of your great knowledge and wisdom, tell us what is the greatest truth you have ever learned?" The great man thought for a minute and tears filled his eyes. Then he said, "I learned the greatest truth at my mother's knee and here it is, 'Jesus loves me, this I know, for the Bible tells me so.'"

This *is* the greatest truth in the world. He loves us, He died for us. And when we put all of our faith in Him we can be assured of eternal life.

### III. The Activities of a Christian

We have been saved through His atoning death, He keeps us and holds us in His hands. Now how is the Christian to live?

1. *He is to live a consecrated Christian life.* He will never be perfect, he will often do and say and think in such a way as to displease God, but he must always try to live at his best. He must try as much as possible to be like Jesus.

Dr. H. Leo Eddleman tells of an Italian woman who was a member of the church of which he was pastor. He said she was the most faithful and most deeply consecrated member of that church. One day he asked her to tell him the secret of her dedicated life. She said, "When I was born my mother did not want me, so she put me in a basket and left that basket by a wall in the town. A couple found me there and took me into their home. When I was fourteen my foster father, who drank heavily, brought me to America. Before long he forced me to become a prostitute to support his drinking. As the months went by my life became more and more miserable. Finally I ran away. Later I met a good man and married him. One day I walked down the street by a church and I heard them singing, 'I was sinking deep in sin, far from the peaceful shore.'

"I went into the church and slipped into a back seat. I heard a man tell about Jesus Christ and how He could wash your sin away and become a great blessing in your life. And when the man invited people to come forward and trust that great Saviour I went forward and gave my life to Jesus. Soon my husband did the same thing. Oh, I have been so happy in Jesus since that time. Do you wonder why I want to give Him my best?" And after all Jesus has done for us, shouldn't we give our best to Him?

2. *He is to give to the Lord's work as God prospers Him.* How much does God say we should give? The Bible tells us that "the tithe is the Lord's." This definitely means that one-tenth of our income does not belong to us. It belongs to God and we have no right to use it for ourselves. We have no right to rob God. He plainly tells us that if we bring our tithes to His storehouse He will pour out such blessings upon us we won't have room to receive them. And every one who has tried God's plan of giving can tell you that God really knows how to pour out the blessings. The faithful tither will soon learn he is able to give more than the tithe, for God will make this possible.

Why do we give our tithes and offerings? We give so that Christ can be made known here and around the world. Our gifts support the local church where men can come and be saved. Then our gifts are used to send others around the world to tell lost men of a great Saviour. The most glorious privilege in life is to have a part in this greatest of all works.

The time had come in a certain church for the members to pledge the budget for the coming year. On a particular Sunday the pastor preached a stewardship sermon. One of his members who came to church about twice a year happened to be present. At the close of the service, when the pastor greeted the members, he asked the man why he didn't come to church more often. The man said, "Every time I come to church I always hear a sermon on giving. Its always give, give, give." And the pastor said, "That's the best definition I ever heard of Christianity. God so loved that He gave His only begotten Son. He gives us everything we have and He'll be giving to us throughout eternity. So He expects us to give our best to Him. Yes, Christianity is all give, give, give." But God gives us a billion times more than we can ever give Him.

3. *He is to tell others of His Saviour.* These are the three activities of a Christian. He lives a consecrated life, always being faithful to God and His church and all of his Christian responsibilities. He gives to the cause of Christ in proportion as God blesses Him. He tells others of the Saviour who has done so much for him, all of the time keeping close to Christ. For the Christian doesn't walk alone, he walks with God.

One outstanding mark of a Christian is that of faithfulness. Jesus said, "Be thou faithful unto death and I will give thee a crown of life." There are crowns here and hereafter for the faithful child of God. In my pastorates I had many faithful members, I knew each Sunday right where they would be sitting. I have gone back twenty or thirty years later and found them right there on the job for God. These are the kind of people who keep the Lord's work going. He does not ask us to be brilliant or learned or powerful, but He does demand that we be faithful and promises a reward for that faithfulness.

### IV. THE ATTAINMENT AT THE END OF THE JOURNEY

At the end of the journey we are going to meet Jesus and hear Him say, "Enter thou into the joys of thy Lord." And that will be the sweetest music these ears have ever heard. That's what it's all about. We strive and strain and struggle here, but Jesus has something better awaiting us. The old preachers used to end every sermon in heaven. That's what I'm going to do. We began by talking about salvation, then assurance, then the activities of a Christian, and my last thoughts will be about heaven.

Suppose there was no sickness in this world, no pain, no trouble, no death, no cemeteries. Suppose there were no harmful drugs, no drunkenness, no crime in this world. Well, heaven is going to be just like that in the presence of Christ with all of God's eternal blessings thrown in.

One night the disciples were on the Sea of Galilee in a small boat when a storm arose. It was dark, they were far from shore, the situation seemed hopeless. Then they saw Jesus walking toward them on the water. They heard Him say, "It is I, be not afraid, I have come to take you home." Today we are tossed about on the waves of trouble and sorrow, but remember, Jesus is coming to take us home just as He said He would.

When I was a little boy I cried a lot, I still do. There are many things that bring tears to my eyes. But I read in Revelation that "God shall wash away all tears from their eyes." And I am looking forward to that time when He calls me home, puts His loving arms around me and wipes away all my tears.

Two men walked down the street by a church. One man said, "I'll bet you $50.00 you won't go in there and make a confession." The other man said, "I'll take you up on that," and he went in and made a fake confession. Then the preacher said to him, "Let me tell you what Jesus did for you." And he told the man the old, old story of Jesus and His death on the cross for sinful men. Then the man went back outside and told his friend what had happened in the church and demanded his $50.00. "Not yet," said his friend, "but go back in there and kneel at the altar and say, 'Jesus, You did all this for me and I couldn't care less,' then I'll pay you off." The man went back into the church, knelt at the altar and said, "Lord, You did all of this for me." Then in a moment he said, "Lord, You did all this for me and I couldn't . . . " and he could get no further. Then he said, "Lord, You did all this for me," and fell upon his face, sobbing out his heart to God and giving himself to Jesus.

Now, as you think of what Christ has done for you, can't you say, "Lord, You did all this for me and now I'll give my best to You"?

# 4.

# Riches That Everyone Can Have

*1 Corinthians 3:21-23*

Everyone of us would like to be wealthy. What would you do if you had a great amount of money? Someone would say, "I would pay off all my debts — the debt on my car, my house, my furniture." Someone else would say, "My present house is getting old, so I would buy a new house." Someone else would say, "I would buy stocks and bonds that would support me in future years." Someone else would say, "I would set my children up in business." Someone else would say, "I would quit work, take life easy, travel around the world." But a devoted Christian would say, "I would use it for Christ, I would build churches and send missionaries and evangelists around the world."

I know some men who are missing the greatest joy in the world. They have money and they keep on striving to get more. But they hold on to it, they use it for themselves. If they used their money for God their lives would overflow with happiness. One day these rich people will die and leave their wealth behind for their relatives to squander or quarrel over. And they themselves will stand before God, only to find that they are poor in the things that really matter.

Christ tells us to lay up our treasures in heaven. There is only one way to do that. We must invest our money in those things that will help get people into heaven. Earthly things will fade away; heavenly things will last forever.

Yes, it would be nice to be rich. I saw a store in Honolulu which rented for $5,000.00 per month. I saw the Shah of Iran, a man who is fabulously rich because of the oil in his country. I heard of a man whose income is $1,000,000.00 per day. Imagine what you could do with all that money.

But I want to talk to you about a different kind of wealth, riches that everyone can have. These are spiritual riches, the riches of the redeemed. Some people believe you must give up everything worthwhile when you become a Christian. They say, "I would be forced to give up my cocktails, my gambling, my worldly companions." But these are not worthwhile things, they have no real value. Wouldn't it be worthwhile to give up a penny to get a thousand dollars? Wouldn't it be worthwhile to give up a piece of glass to get a diamond? Then how much more worthwhile to give up our worldly indulgences to gain Christ and heaven!

Jesus said, "Behold I stand at the door and knock." He wants to come in and dine with you. He wants to come into your life and bring you the best things of two worlds. He wants to take out of your life all that is poisonous and hurtful and fill that life with everything good.

A father stood upon a high hill with his son and pointed to all of the land on every side and said to his son, "All this is yours, I am giving it to you." In our text Paul stands upon the peak of inspiration and says, "Christian, all these things are yours."

## I. Six Things Which Belong to the Christian

1. *The ministry belongs to the Christian.* The people in Corinth were divided, some liked one preacher, some another. Paul says that all preachers are theirs and ours, each one could bring a special blessing. Some of the Corinthians would say, "I like Paul. He is so logical, he preaches doc-

trine, he gives me the meat of the Word." Some would say, "I like Apollos, he is a great orator, he lifts me to the sky, he stirs my soul." Some would say, "I like Simon Peter. He touches my heart, he makes me cry. Yet he is such a comforting preacher."

The text says all preachers are yours, they are here to serve you. When you have sorrow they are here to comfort, when you have problems they are here to advise, when you are seeking salvation, they are here to guide you. The true preacher always wants to serve people in the Name of Christ.

When you need a preacher don't hesitate to call on him. Some church members go to a hospital and stay there a couple of weeks, but they never notify the pastor. Then they blame the pastor for not coming to see them. This isn't fair to him. So be sure to notify the pastor when you need him. He stands "among you as one who serves."

2. *The world belongs to the Christian.* Why did God put so much beauty in the world? He put it there for His children to enjoy. The mountains are yours, you go to them for health and to feel the cool breezes. The sea is yours, you go to it to rest and swim and as you watch the waves they seem to speak peace to your spirits. The trees, the grass, the flowers, they are all yours to enjoy. The famous places of the world, Niagara Falls, the Grand Canyon, the great redwood forests, they are all yours to enjoy.

3. *Life belongs to the Christian.* So says Paul in our text. Now this is a life that never ends. "He that believeth on the Son hath everlasting life" (John 3:36).

(1) *In this life there is peace.* The man without Christ has no peace. But the Christian has had his sins forgiven and he has peace in his heart. He is ready to live and ready to die.

Two artists painted pictures expressing their ideas of peace. One picture was a beautiful scene at eventide beside a placid lake. The trees, the grass, the quietude, all were sweet expressions of peace. But the other artist painted a picture of a raging storm. Black clouds filled the sky, turbulent waters poured over a precipice. But under the waterfall there was an overhanging rock and under that rock was a bird's nest. A mother bird and her little ones rested safely and snugly in the nest.

The latter picture depicts real peace. No life is without trouble, no life is always calm and quiet. But the artist was saying that peace comes amid the storms of life when we are safe in Christ, the Eternal Rock.

> Rock of ages, cleft for me,
> Let me hide myself in Thee;
> Let the water and the blood,
> From Thy wounded side which flowed,
> Be of sin the double cure,
> Save from wrath and make me pure.
>
> Could my tears forever flow,
> Could my zeal no languor know,
> These for sin could not atone;
> Thou must save, and Thou alone;
> In my hand no price I bring,
> Simply to Thy cross I cling.
>
> While I draw this fleeting breath,
> When mine eyes shall close in death,
> When I rise to worlds unknown,
> And behold Thee on Thy throne,
> Rock of Ages, cleft for me,
> Let me hide myself in Thee.

Augustus M. Toplady

(2) *In this life there is joy.* Someone asked a great musician why his sacred music was so buoyant and full of joy. And he replied, "That is the way I feel. When I think of God my heart sings with joy." So when you come to Christ

He gives you a joy the world cannot give nor take away. He lifts you up, puts your feet on a rock and a new song on your lips.

4. *Death belongs to the Christian.* Did you ever think of death as your servant? That's the way it is pictured in our text. It is a servant who comes and says, "I have come to release you into a fuller, better, richer life." Death is not a servant of the sinner. It means the end of all of his joy and the beginning of an eternity of sorrow and bitter agony.

Here is a child who goes over to a neighbor's house. They mistreat him over there. They beat him, they slap him, the dog bites him. Don't you think he would be glad when a servant comes to take him home? Well, that's the way it is with us. The world is not the Christian's friend. It knocks him, disappoints him. So death the servant is welcome when it comes to release the Christian from all the woes of the world.

5. *The things present belong to the Christian.* This surely means that a Christian can find happiness in this world. May the Lord deliver us from a religion that has no joy in it. I read of a convent in one of our Southern states. The monks go there to spend a lifetime. They work on the farm and in the gardens of the convent. But there is one unusual thing about them — they are never allowed to speak. That is not normal and natural and not according to true Christianity. Theirs is a religion of gloom and sadness.

I am glad Christians can enjoy their religion. They can laugh and joke and still be good Christians. Heaven itself is not a place of gloom, but a place of light and joy and singing. Jesus said, "I am come that ye might have life, and that they might have it more abundantly" (John 10:10).

6. *The things to come belong to the Christian.* This means heaven and all of its joys. They are ours in Christ

Jesus. Are you having a hard time? Look up, heaven is yours. Does sin beset you on every side? Look up, you'll never be tempted in heaven. Do you have trouble here, is it hard to make both ends meet? Look up, He cares for you. Do you long to see those loved ones whom you "have loved long since and lost a while"? Look up, you'll see them one day. Do you sometimes lose the sense of the presence of Christ? Look up, all things in heaven and earth are yours and you'll soon see Him face to face.

## II. One Thing Which Does Not Belong to the Christian

It's in the text. The Christian doesn't belong to himself. "And ye are Christ's," Paul states. We belong to Christ. He bought us one day long ago when He shed His blood on a cross for us.

1. *Since we are His, we'll never be lost.* The great and powerful Saviour never loses one of His own. When you come unto God through Christ you become a child of God and no child of God will ever go to hell.

Sometimes a Christian thinks of his past sins and worries about them. Satan says to him, "Look at the sins of your life, don't you know you are not fit to go to heaven?" Then we remember that "the blood of Jesus Christ his Son cleanseth us from all sin." So we can say to Satan, "Go and see Jesus about those sins, He is taking care of them."

One day the oceans may run dry, the mountains may crumble into the dust, the sun may burn out. But the soul who has trusted Christ will live on and on in heaven with Him forever while all the ages roll on.

2. *Since we are His we ought to live like it.* A group of slaves was being driven to their tasks one morning. They stumbled along with their heads down, beaten, defeated, hopeless. But one young man walked with head held high and a spring in his step. When someone asked why he did

this the answer came, "He is the son of an African king and he never forgets it." You and I as Christians are sons of the heavenly King, so we ought to lift our lives above the sin of the world and live in such a way that others will know we belong to Jesus.

Some years ago I was on a ship coming from Hawaii. I had the privilege of preaching on the ship on Sunday morning. That night a woman who had heard me preach asked me if I would be going into the lounge to play bingo. When I told her I was not going to do this, she said, "Neither am I, but my husband who is a deacon in his home church and who teaches a Sunday school class lives a little different- ly when he is away from home, so he is in there." The next morning I learned the man had won $85.00. But I say that Christians, at home and abroad, ought to live better lives than worldlings.

3. *Since we are His we ought to be busy for Him.* He has no hands but our hands to do His work. If we fail, His churches will close, missionaries will be brought home, souls will be lost and all our ministries to the unfortunate will cease.

Maybe you have been saying, "I know I ought to be busy for Christ, I know His work is the only work that counts, someday I'll get busy for Him." But that "someday" never comes. The days are passing, the night cometh when no man can work. Why not get busy for Him now?

Let us imagine a scene in heaven, You stand before the Saviour, you see Him in all of His glory, you realize at last all He did for you in dying for you, in saving you, in bring- ing you home to heaven. Then He says to you, "You were on the way to hell, weren't you?" And you will answer, "Yes, Lord." "Now," He will say, "you had a lifetime to serve Me, but you gave all of your time to the world. Why didn't you serve the Saviour who died for you?" And you won't be able to say one word, you will stand ashamed in the presence of the Lord. Do you want that to happen to you? Why not get busy for Him?

4. *Since we are His we will someday see Him face to face.* A certain blind man was groping his way through the world. One day a specialist said to him, "I believe I can operate and give you your sight." The operation was performed and the day came when the bandages were to be removed. When they were taken off, the man opened his eyes and then quickly closed them. "I would like to see my doctor first of all," he said. The doctor stood before him and the man fell at the doctor's feet and thanked him for what he had done for him.

And surely, when we get to heaven and rejoice in our heavenly eyesight, we will want to see our Saviour first of all. He left heaven for us, He came into a hostile world for us, He loved us and died for us and saved us. Surely we'll want to fall at His feet and thank Him for it all.

So remember this — if you are a Christian you are never poor. All good things in Christ are yours, now and in the sweet bye-and-bye of heaven. But remember that you belong to Jesus and live for Him every day.

One night in San Francisco at a Billy Graham meeting I listened to the testimony of an Englishman named John French. He had been an actor and he said that at one time he hated the Bible and Christ and Billy Graham and all he stood for. After reading an article written by Dr. Graham he said, "Tommyrot, if I ever see him I'll punch him in the nose." A friend took him to a press conference where Graham was slated to speak. He said, "I got ready to punch him in the nose but when I confronted him he stuck out his hand and said, 'I am praying for you.'" Then he met Cliff Barrows and he said, "I am praying for you." Then Mr. French said, "Why are they praying for me? I go to church twice every year and I have never killed anyone." As he listened to Billy Graham he became disturbed about himself, so he went home and read the account of the crucifixion. He realized finally that Christ loved him and had died for him. He then made an appointment with Graham, saying, "I know now that I need Jesus." Soon he was gloriously saved.

When he want back to his room he read John 5:24. In his testimony he said, "Thank God, Jesus was talking about me. I know I have passed from death unto life. Three years have passed now and God blesses me every day. Christ lives within and I know Christianity works."

Yes, thank God you and I have a Saviour, He's wonderful, He loves us, He walks with us, He's taking us to heaven. Don't you think we ought to be more faithful to Him?

# 5.

# Spiritual Vitamins for Growing Souls

## 2 Peter 3:10-18

I have made several trips through Carlsbad Caverns in New Mexico and other caverns in America. As one goes through these caverns the guide explains the various geological formations. First, there are the stalactites, hard columns which grow downward from the top of the cave. Then there are the stalagmites, hard columns which grow upward from the base of the cave. The guide will tell you these columns grow only one inch in every hundred years. That isn't much growth, but it is natural growth.

It is natural for every living thing to grow. The woodsman can tell you the age of a tree by the rings which grow around the trunk of the tree. We are told that the great Redwood trees of California were hundreds of years old when Christ was born. It is natural for trees and flowers to grow, it is natural for people to grow, it is natural for souls to grow. If there is anything that saddens the heart of Jesus, it is the stunted condition of His children.

Yonder is a little home and in that home there is a young woman who is looking forward to the coming of her first baby. One day she goes to the hospital and slips down into the valley of motherhood to bring that child into the world. When the little one is laid by her side she looks up to God and whispers, "Thank You, dear Lord." The child seems to be healthy and grows physically from day to day. But he doesn't seem to be beware of his surroundings and nothing claims his attention. Finally the parents reach the heartbreaking conclusion that he is definitely mentally retarded. They lavish their affection upon him but there is no improvement. He grows to be a strong man physically but he hardly even knows his father and mother. They carry their grief everywhere because there has been no growth mentally. The full-grown man has the mind of a little child.

That is a sad thing but there is something sadder. One day you were on the road to hell. But God saved you, He plucked you as a brand from the burning. That was a happy day for you. You made some high and holy vows to God and He counted on you to keep those vows, He expected you to grow in grace and become a better Christian with the passing days. But you disappointed Him, you haven't grown any. You are content simply to have your name on the roll, you don't mean much to God or to His church.

Jesus pleased God because of His growth. "He increased in wisdom and stature and in favor with God and man" (Luke 2:52). No wonder God said, "This is my beloved Son in whom I am well pleased" (Matt. 3:17).

In our text Peter tells us all Christians should grow in grace. For a person to grow physically he must eat physical food. We are told that certain vitamins benefit our physical health and help to ward off certain diseases. And if a soul is to grow that soul must have certain spiritual vitamins. Let us look at some of the spiritual vitamins necessary for our spiritual development.

## I. First Vitamin — Prayer

Prayer is the vital breath of a Christian, he can't grow without it. It is his principal spiritual food. Even Jesus needed to pray, how much more do we. Yet the sad fact is that Christians pray very little.

In the United States capital there is a spot where one can whisper and that whisper is easily heard a hundred or more feet away. Oh, but God hears better than that, He hears every whisper of the heart.

A praying man is never defeated. God promises him victory, and supplies his every need. The great English preacher, Spurgeon, took a man through his orphanage where more than five hundred children were being cared for. When the man asked Spurgeon how he was able to finance such a big enterprise, Spurgeon said, "Yonder is the bank where I get the money." "I don't see any bank," the man said. "Look over the door," said Spurgeon. And the man saw a carving over the door which read, "Jehovah-Jireh," which means "The Lord will provide." All the great resources of God are ours if we ask for them in faith and use them for God's glory. God is a most generous Father. He gives us more air than we need, more water than we can consume, more stars than any man can number.

When a little girl was being put to bed she said, "Wait a minute, mother, I forgot my soul." So she got out of bed, knelt down and said her simple child's prayer. Yes, we remember so much today but we forget our souls, the spiritual side of our natures. We seldom lift our voices in prayer.

But the deepest prayers are not always expressed in spoken words. They are found in the opening of our souls to God. Our hearts flow out to Him and His love flows down to us. We are told He will give if we ask in faith, believing. But prayer also has a reflex action, it not only brings an answer from God, but it blesses and enriches the one who prays. The soul grows and is drawn closer to God. As the body cannot do without physical food, as the flowers cannot do without sunshine and rain, so the growing soul cannot exist without prayer.

## II. Second Vitamin — Bible Study

Let me say two things — I never saw a great Christian who didn't study his Bible and I never saw a man who studied the Bible who did not grow into a stronger and better Christian. Every home has a Bible, it is a best-seller. But in the average home it is seldom touched. Dust on the Bible means blight on the soul.

When a certain young man went away to college his father gave him a Bible and told him to be sure to read the eighth chapter of Romans. The time came when the boy turned to that chapter and found not only a blessing for his heart, but a fifty-dollar bill the father had placed there for him. Yes, there are riches in the Word of God for all who will read it.

My wife had an uncle who lived in Nashville, Tennessee. His neighbor's house was close to his own and that neighbor said that on summer nights when their windows were open they could hear my wife's uncle reading the Bible to his wife. When he died I was called on to assist in conducting his funeral. His pastor described him as one of the greatest Christians he had ever known. No wonder, he had read the Word of God and patterned his life after its teachings. All of us ought to take time to study God's Book.

## III. Third Vitamin — Daily Confession of Sin

When you come to Christ and take Him as your Saviour and Lord, you confess your sin and forsake it. But the battle has just begun. Satan is going to tempt you on all sides. Every day you will fail the Lord in some way. You will sin in some measure. Then you will need to confess that sin, to pour out your heart to God in penitence. In this way only can you keep the channel clear between you and God. You ought never to go to sleep at night until you have straightened things out with God.

Some of you have not confessed your sins to God in a long time. They have piled up until they stand today between you and God. You need to fall on your face before Him and cry out for forgiveness. Will He hear and forgive? We have His word that He will. "If we confess our sins, he is faithful and just to forgive us our sins, and to cleanse us from all unrighteousness" (1 John 1:9). You confess your sins and as sure as the sun shines by day and the stars by night, just as sure as the rivers run to the sea and the mountains lift their heads toward heaven, just as sure as there is a God, He will forgive you.

I remember a golf course where I played a few times in my younger days. There was a slight rise above the fifth hole and on this rise there was a cool, clear sparkling mountain spring. So someone ran a pipe-line down from the spring to the golf course. Then when anyone came to the fifth hole, he could be assured of a cool drink. One fall day I stopped for a drink but no water came through the pipeline. Then I found that the autumn leaves had fallen into the spring and stopped up the pipeline. When I removed the leaves the spring came running down to the golf course. In like manner sin often stops up the channel between us and God. But confession keeps the channel clear, so to keep the communication and blessing line flowing down to us from God, there must be a constant confession of sin. We never grow as Christians unless we confess our sins.

## IV. FOURTH VITAMIN — CHURCH ATTENDANCE

When your pastor urges you to come to church it is not just to get a crowd. He knows the power of the Gospel, he knows that the sermons and the songs and the prayers will help to make you a better person. I believe so much in the power of the Gospel that I want to make what to you may seem to be a startling statement. I believe that if 100 lost people attended church faithfully for six months where they heard a true gospel preacher, 80 of them would be saved. And I believe that if 100 cold, indifferent Christians did the same thing, the majority of them would be revived.

I have seen men who were nominal church members, who had never grown in grace. Then for some reason they began to attend church and I watched the transforming power of the Gospel of Christ as their lives were radically changed. It is never easy to live the Christian life, but it is made much easier when one goes to church every Sunday.

Some years ago I was in New York City over the week-end. Certain circumstances so worked against me that I didn't get to church in the morning until they were singing the invitation hymn at the close of the service. Then at night I lost the way and missed another service. As I retired to the hotel that night I was really depressed. I felt that the day had been wasted. I had an empty feeling that only the Gospel could have filled. And now I wonder how Christians can go week after week without going to church.

You may not be able to preach or sing a solo or teach a Bible class, but there is one thing you can do. You can be in your place in God's house at every service. Your faithfulness will not only be a blessing to your own heart, but it will greatly influence others for Christ.

### V.  FIFTH VITAMIN — MEDITATION

Most of us are too busy to stop and think about God's goodness to us, but we would be better people if we took some time to meditate on these things. Think of the salvation He has given you, think of His daily blessings and care, think of His mercies that are new every morning. Then think of the vows you have made to God. Have you kept those vows? You need to meditate on all these things.

But what do we have on our minds today? Things, things, things! Material things. God and His goodness are forgotten. Jesus tells of a man who made a bumper crop one year.

But he forgot about God's part in it — he thought only of himself. "I, I, I," he kept on saying. But his soul couldn't feed on these material things, it cried out for spiritual food.

The Lord says, "Be still and know that I am God" (Ps. 46:10). Why not try this exercise? Sit down and think of God, think of what He is like, think of all He has done for you. Before you have been thinking very long, you will begin to thank Him for being your Father and allowing you to be His child. The right kind of thinking always leads to thanking.

Oh, that all of us had more time, that we could leave off all our rushing and striving and let our hearts dwell on God.

## VI. Sixth Vitamin — Christian Activity

Just as a physical body needs exercise for physical growth, so does the soul need spiritual activity for spiritual growth. There are people who have been Christians for many years, but they haven't grown much because they haven't engaged in any Christian activity.

You always get out of a thing just what you put into it. A preacher took his little boy out to a country church where he was scheduled to preach. As they entered the vestibule the preacher noticed an offering box so he dropped a quarter in it. At the close of the service the church treasurer said, "We always give our visiting preacher all the money we find in the offering box." So he opened up the box and gave the preacher the total offering — one quarter. As they left the church the little boy said, "Papa, if you had put more in it, you would have gotten more out of it, wouldn't you?" That's true also in the spiritual realm. We get out of it what we put into it.

A rich man showed his friend some precious stones, saying, "They are beautiful but they don't yield any income." The other man said, "Let me show you two stones. They are not very pretty, they cost very little, yet they yield a good income." And he showed him two toiling gray mill-stones, working for their master. God has many people who look good, but they are doing nothing. He would be more pleased if they were working for Him.

When John the Baptist became inactive, when he was in prison, he began to have doubts about Jesus. When David became idle he sank down into deepest sin. Get busy for God and doubts will fly and the temptations not be as great.

A vital part of our Christian activity is our giving. God says the tithe belongs to Him. What a joy to come to His house each Lord's day, ready to place His tithes in His work! The happy Christians are those who have learned God's plan of giving.

### VII. SEVENTH VITAMIN — SOULWINNING

If you have been saved it is God's plan for you to tell others. There are hundreds of lost people around us who never come to church to hear a saving Gospel. They'll never be won to Christ unless they see Jesus in your life and hear about Him from your lips.

Dr. L. R. Scarborough conducted the funeral of a young man and he noticed an older man who was weeping and seemed to be deeply grieved. At the close of the service, Dr. Scarborough asked the man, "Were you related to this young man?" He answered through his tears, "No, but he worked for me for six years. I am a deacon, I knew he was not a Christian, but I never spoke to him about his salvation."

Some years ago I conducted a revival in a Georgia town. There was a fire station across the street from the church. The captain of the station was not a Christian. The pastor and I visited him and invited him to the meeting. He came several nights and listened attentively to my sermons. Then one night after church we took him into the pastor's study to talk to him about his salvation. That night he gave his heart to Christ and the next night he walked forward and made his public profession of faith. A few days later he had to fight a big warehouse fire. After he returned to the fire station he came over to the church and said to us. "In other days I was afraid the burning embers might fall upon me or a wall might collapse and crush me. But I was not afraid this time, because I had my best Friend, Jesus, with me." Oh, life becomes more worthwhile when you know that your efforts have helped someone to know that Friend.

You may not be able to take your Bible and sit down with someone and talk about salvation to him, but at least you can invite him to come to church and hear the Gospel. The Bible says people cannot be saved until they hear the Word, so it's up to you to invite them.

Someday you are going to face the great Saviour. He will say, "I left heaven's glory for you, I came down to earth's shame for you, I died on a cruel cross for you. What did you do for Me?" Must you say, "Lord, I did nothing for You, I was too busy about other things, now I am empty handed"? Or are you living in such a way that when you get home you'll hear Him say, "Well done, thou good and faithful servant"?

Some years ago a ship was wrecked off the Irish coast, resulting in the loss of several lives. The captain and the crew were careful and experienced sailors, the weather was not too bad. Yet the ship was blown off its course and into the rocks. Why? When the divers went down to investigate the wreck they brought the compass out. Upon close examination they found the broken blade of a knife stuck in the compass. The blade had lodged there when a sailor was cleaning the compass.

That little piece of steel threw the compass off and caused the shipwreck. And there are many Christians who ought to be sailing on course for Jesus, living for Him and serving

Him. But they let some sin or the world come in their lives and they get off course, often running aground. If this is true of you, may God help you to fall at His feet, confess your sins, make a full surrender to Him and receive the power He wants you to have.

So let us partake of these seven vitamins:

1. Prayer
2. Bible Study
3. Daily Confession
4. Church Attendance
5. Meditation
6. Christian Activity and Tithing
7. Soulwinning

These vitamins will help to make you a strong Christian, the Christian God wants you to be.

# 6.

# The Greatest Question Ever Asked

*Matthew 27:22*

The Bible contains some great questions. In the garden of Eden after our first parents had disobeyed God and brought sin into the world, we hear the Lord saying, "Adam, where art thou?" Later we hear God saying to Cain, after Cain had slain Abel, "Where is thy brother?" Then we hear Job asking the question, "If a man die, shall he live again?" The Philippian jailer asked Paul and Silas a great question, "What must I do to be saved?" Jesus asked this question of the Pharisees, "What think ye of Christ? Whose Son is he?"

These are all great questions and life is filled with many other great questions. But the greatest question any man will ever be called on to answer is the question of my text. Pilate asked it, "What shall I do then with Jesus which is called Christ?" Let us look at the background of this question. The Lord Jesus had been arrested, He had been kept up all night, He had been shifted from one court to another. He had been beaten and spat upon, crowned with a crown of thorns, humiliated and degraded. Now in the early morning He stands before Governor Pilate. Pilate knew Jesus was innocent, for he had said, "I find no fault in Him." Mrs. Pilate had said to her husband, "I dreamed about this man last night. He is a good man, don't have anything to do with hurting Him."

But Pilate was a petty politician, an opportunist. He was not concerned with the right or wrong of his actions, he wanted only the favor of the people. The mob cried out, "Let Him (Jesus) be crucified." Pilate knew that Jesus was an innocent man, but he wanted to please the crowd. So he decided to try one more plan. He went out upon his balcony, taking Jesus with him and a notorious criminal named Barabbas. Pilate then said to the crowd, "You know my custom, on this feast day I always release a prisoner. You are to choose the one I am to set free. Here is Barabbas, you know his criminal record. And here is the one called Jesus Christ, you know about Him. Which one shall I release unto you?" And the mob cried out, "Release Barabbas." Then Pilate asked this important question, "What shall I do then with Jesus which is called Christ?" And the cry came back, "Let Him be crucified." Then Pilate asked another question, "Why, what evil hath He done?" But they cried out even louder, "Let Him be crucified." So Pilate turned Jesus over to the soldiers to be crucified.

This is the most important question ever asked or answered. Every person born into the world must answer it. God says to every man, "I gave My Son for you, what are you going to do with Him?" Everything, yes, everything in this world and the next depends upon your answer.

Let us call in several people and ask them the question, "What did you do with Jesus?"

### I. We Call Judas

"Judas," we say, "tell us something about yourself." And he answers, "I lived here in Judah, I heard John the Baptist preach, I heard him tell about the coming Messiah. Then on a certain day I heard Jesus preach. I was strangely moved and I decided to leave my old life and follow Him. He took me in as one of His disciples, and because of my business experience He made me treasurer of His group." (You will note, however, that in every list of the disciples the name of Judas always comes last.)

Judas continues, "For three-and-a-half years I went everywhere with Him. I heard Him preach, I saw Him perform mighty miracles, I walked and talked with Him." Now the question arises in our minds. Jesus knew everything, He could see deep into the hearts of men. Why did He choose Judas when He knew that Satan ruled Judas and that he would betray Him? This is a mystery that will be unraveled for us only in eternity. But we can learn a valuable lesson right here. Judas lived close to holy things, yet he had an unregenerate heart that was never changed.

So today it isn't enough for a man to go to church, join in the singing and drop some money into the offering plate. He can do all this and be lost and spend eternity in hell. Something must happen on the inside, he must be born again, he must have the experience of salvation. Outside culture and good works are not enough.

Well, how did Judas answer this great question? He gave the wrong answer and lost everything. He carried the bag of money and as the contributions became larger he was tempted to steal and probably did so. We know that he had a covetous heart, for when Mary broke open the alabaster box and poured the ointment upon Jesus, Judas said, "Why not sell this ointment for 300 pence and give it to the poor?" Then we read that he didn't care for the poor, but wanted the money for himself.

Before long we see Judas at another supper. Jesus is at the center with His disciples all about Him. Jesus prophesied that one of them would betray Him. Then the question went the rounds, "Lord, is it I?" Jesus pointed out Judas as the guilty one and said to him, "What thou doest, do quickly." Then Judas went out and "it was night."

Oh, friend, it is always night when one goes out from Christ. They go out into the night of sin, of misery, of unhappiness, they go out into the night of hell and eternal torment.

Let's follow Judas. Where does he go? He goes to the enemies of Jesus and sells Him out for 30 pieces of silver, the price of a slave. And how was Judas to identify Jesus? It was by means of a kiss. Think of it, a kiss is supposed to be the mark of love but Judas used it to betray the Son of God. Later that night Jesus and the disciples came out of the Garden of Prayer. Then Judas leads the mob up to Jesus, steps forward and kisses the Lord on the cheek. Then the mob rushes Jesus off to trial and to death.

But what became of Judas? The money burned his pocket, his hands, his soul. So he took it back to the enemies of Christ and called out, "Let's rue the bargain, I have betrayed innocent blood." They just laughed at him, so poor old Judas went into a garden and committed suicide. And his name down over the centuries has come to mean all that is low and base.

Judas answered this great question wrongly. He did the wrong thing with Jesus. Today men are still selling Jesus out. In their eagerness to gain worldly possessions which last for this life only they give up Jesus and the wealth that lasts forever.

Once a saloon owner and his wife went to church and heard a great sermon on the text, "For what shall it profit a man, if he shall gain the whole world, and lose his own soul?" The man was strangely moved by the gospel message. On the way home his wife said to him, "How much do you make clear from the saloon each year?" He replied, "About $5,000." Then she asked, "How many more years do you expect to remain in business?" He answered, "About 20 years." Then she said, "That would mean you would make $100,000. Are you willing to sell your soul for $100,000?" He replied, "No, it is worth more than that." He turned his back on his saloon and gave his heart to Christ.

If you gain a billion dollars and lose your soul and go to hell, you'll be making a bad, bad bargain. Poor old Judas made the worst bargain any man ever made.

## II. WE CALL PILATE

We ask Pilate to tell us something about himself and he says, "I am a Roman citizen. Sometime ago I was appointed governor of Judea by Caesar, the great emperor. I have a good job with a good salary. I live in a fine palace and I am attended by many servants. My big trouble here is with the Jews. Of course, they don't like us Romans because we occupy their country and levy heavy taxes upon them. So they are always stirring up trouble."

"Go ahead, Pilate, what else?" And he says, "Here lately I have heard of a man called Jesus. He seems to be a good man and I hear that he has done some wonderful things. But the majority of the Jews hate Him and want me to have Him crucified. This morning my wife said to me, 'Last night I dreamed about this man, Jesus. Please don't get mixed up in this affair. He is a good man, please don't have anything to do with harming Him.'"

But Pilate can't be neutral, he can't leave Jesus alone. Christ is brought before him and he must make a decision. "Pilate, what are you going to do with Jesus who is called Christ? You know He is innocent. He doesn't deserve death." But Pilate, even though he knows all this, wants to please the Jews.

I can imagine the high priest saying to Pilate in oily tones, "Governor, you have a good job here, the best job you have ever had. I have seen governors come and go. You know that Caesar feels he is God, but this Jesus says He is God. If you release Him you are going to displease Caesar and lose your governorship. You know what that means, Pilate. You will be banished to the mines of Patmos. Down there you will be forced to work long hours, there will be callouses on your hands, your back will bend and your hair turn gray, you'll eat black bread and vermin will crawl over you at night. You'd better be smart, Pilate. You don't want to exchange your soft life in the palace for a bleak life on Patmos. What is your decision, Pilate, will you crucify Jesus for us or go into exile?"

And right then Pilate sealed himself in hell forever. He decided against Christ and in favor of wealth and ease and position and ordered that Jesus be crucified. The trouble with Pilate is that he couldn't see beyond the present. He thought only of a few years of ease here, he didn't think of the time when Christ would judge him.

Why do so many people today turn Christ down? It is because they are more interested in this world than in the future. They forget that we live here just for a few years and then throughout eternity in another world. They forget that they must face the judgment bar of God. They forget that to leave Christ out means eternal hell. Oh, friend, remember that this world soon fades away for us all and that our only hope for the life to come is in Christ. Like Pilate, you seal yourself in hell if you choose anything over Christ.

Pilate took a basin of water and washed his hands, saying, "I am washing my hands of the blood of this innocent man." But that was an empty gesture. The guilt was not on his hands, but on his soul forever. An artist of another day pictures Pilate in hell washing his hands and crying out in anguish, "Oh, will they never be clean, will they never be clean?" If you turn down Jesus as Pilate did you will also be crying out in hell. You will say, "I had my chance on earth, I heard the Gospel, I felt the call of the Holy Spirit. But I held on to my sin, I put off the matter of my salvation and now I am lost forever."

One of the hottest flames of hell will be that of a burning conscience. It will torment the lost man forever. How awful it will be to be shut up in hell, remembering always that you didn't have to go there. George Eliot tells of a young unmarried woman who hid the body of her new-born baby in a hedgerow. She found a home later a few miles away with an elderly couple. She said nothing about the baby but her conscience made her miserable. Then one night a storm swept the valley, the rains fell and the winds blew. The girl ran out of the house screaming, "My baby, my baby, I hear the cries of my baby." No, she didn't hear the cries of her baby, she heard the voice of her own conscience. It is awful to have a burning conscience here. How much worse to have one throughout all eternity. Only Christ can cure a troubled conscience.

Pilate answered the great question, "What shall I do with Christ?", in the wrong way. Now he is forever lost because of it.

### III. We Call the Mob

We ask that howling mob, "What are you going to do with Christ?" And they cry out, "Let Him be crucified, and let His blood be upon us and upon our children."

They said that they would take the blame and bear the punishment, if it was to come. And history records that God's righteous judgment came upon that nation. In a few years their beloved city of Jerusalem was destroyed and Israel ceased to be a nation. Now the Jews have been driven to every corner of the world, they have been unmercifully persecuted, millions of them were brutally slain in Germany. Why did all this trouble come upon them? They asked for it, they said, "Let the blame rest upon us and our children."

Now you can't trust a mob, a crowd. The least little thing will upset them and cause them to do something which the individual members would regret in the quieter moments of individual contemplation. So in answering the question as to what you will do with Jesus you must forget the crowd. You are an individual, you are born alone, you live alone, you die alone, you go before God alone. You must forget what people will say, whoever they may be, and answer aright the question, "What shall I do with Jesus?"

Back in the ancient days of Rome a certain ruler had an ambitious daughter. She wanted to be the ruler so she hired cruel men to kill her father so she could succeed to the throne. After she heard that he was dead she got in a chariot to ride to the palace and take his place. At one place in the road the horses shied to one side for they saw a dead body on one side of the road. The driver told the young woman that it was the body of her father. Instead of getting out of the chariot and weeping over the body and giving her father a decent burial, she commanded the driver to drive on to the palace.

That is the attitude of the crowds today. They rush on to pleasure, sin, wealth, position, caring nothing for Jesus and passing Him by. Oh, don't follow the crowd, decide for yourself, decide in favor of Christ.

If we had time we could ask many others how they felt about Jesus. We could ask Peter and he would say, "I loved Him and gave my life for Him, He is most precious." We could ask Paul and he would say, "I was the chief of sinners but He came into my life and saved me. Now I know whom I have believed and am persuaded that He is able to keep that which I have committed unto Him." We could ask John and hear him say, "I gave my heart to Him and He became my all in all, my bright and morning star."

### IV. WHAT WILL YOU DO WITH JESUS?

1. *What can you do with Jesus?* You can accept Him or reject Him, you can be for Him or against Him. You may say, "I will neither accept Him or reject Him, I will do nothing with Him." But there is no neutral ground, if you are not for Him you are against Him.

At a certain meeting a little card was handed out to all

who attended. On one side the question was asked, "What must I do to be saved?" And the answer was given, "Believe on the Lord Jesus Christ and thou shalt be saved." On the other side this question was asked, "What must I do to be lost?" And the answer was simply, "Nothing." That's it. You don't have to be a drunkard or a murderer or an adulterer to be lost. Just leave Jesus Christ out of your life and you'll be lost forever.

2. *Who can answer this question for you?* You are the only one. The preacher can't answer it for you, your parents can't answer it for you, your friends can't answer it for you. I have had mothers come to me and say, "Please pray for my boy, I am so anxious to see him saved." Don't you know that if she could do it she would gladly answer "yes" to Jesus for that boy. But each one must answer this question for himself.

And it won't be God's fault if you answer this question in the wrong way. He has done everything to save you. He puts a thousand things in your pathway to warn you and point you to the Saviour. He sends preachers with their sermons, He gives you a guidebook, the Holy Bible. He plants gospel churches everywhere, He moves your conscience, He works upon your better judgment. He gives you a mother who prays for you, He sends sorrows to bring you to Him, He sends the Holy Spirit to convict you of your sin and your need of Christ. If you pass by all of these and go to hell, throughout all eternity you will know it was your own fault and not God's.

3. *What does it matter as to what you do with Jesus?*

(1) *Your happiness here depends upon it.* A man can never be really happy as long as he is without Christ and on the way to hell. He can never be happy with worldly fame and fortune as long as his sin stands between him and God.

Lord Clive was the founder of the British-Indian Empire. His father wrote to him, saying, "Son, hurry home, the nation is wild over your success." He came back to England and was given a peerage. A ceaseless stream of gold poured into his purse, people bowed before him and applauded him wherever he went. Yet, with that applause ringing in his ears he went up into the garret, put a pistol to his head and committed suicide. It takes more than men's applause to make a man happy, it takes Jesus in the heart.

(2) *Your usefulness and influence depend upon what you do with Jesus.* No man ever rises to his highest and best unless he is a Christian. The men who make the greatest contribution to life are those who live for Christ.

(3) *Your eternal destiny depends upon what you do with Jesus.* Eternity is forever and forever, where are you going to spend it? If you leave Christ out of your life you'll spend it in hell, if you take Him as your Saviour you'll spend it in heaven.

Aaron Burr served as a vice-president of the United States, but he is best remembered as the man who killed Alexander Hamilton, our first secretary of the treasury, in a duel. When Aaron Burr was in college a revival broke out and many students were saved. Aaron went to one of his professors and asked if he should become a Christian at that time or wait until the revival fires died out. The professor said, "Aaron, there is only one time to accept Christ and that time is now." Aaron left the room, saying, "I'll come back tonight with my answer." Then he went to another teacher, a cold, unemotional man. This teacher told him not to become a Christian during the revival but to wait until some quiet Sunday morning.

Late that night Burr went back to the first professor and said, "I have been walking up and down the campus, thinking about this matter of becoming a Christian. And just before I came up the steps I clenched my fist toward heaven and said, 'Jesus, Son of God, if You will let me alone and never come back to me, I'll let You alone.'" And Aaron rushed out into the night and into historical infamy.

Fifty years later a dedicated personal worker approached Burr and said to him, "Sir, are you a Christian?" "No, young man, my name is Aaron Burr." Then he told the story of his decision years before and ended up by saying, "From that day Jesus has never knocked at the door of my heart again."

Oh, the tragedy of saying "No" to Jesus. It is tragic for time and eternity. Please don't say "no" to Him. Won't you say, "Come into my heart, Lord Jesus, take my sin away and save me"?

# 7.

# God Is Able

*Hebrews* 7:25

The man who limits God simply does not know God. That man reads the Bible and says, "I don't believe that, it just couldn't happen." But with God all things are possible, He has all power in heaven and earth. Someone says, "I have read about miracles, but they just don't happen in this modern age." But that great woman of faith, Kathryn Kuhlman, begins her television program each week by saying, "I believe in miracles because I believe in God." There's the answer right there.

For instance, Sennacherib and his mighty army came up against Hezekiah the king of Judah. Sennacherib sent an insulting letter to Hezekiah. In it he said, "You trust in your God, but we care not for all He can do for you. We have destroyed other nations who trusted in their gods and we'll destroy you." Now what did Hezekiah do? He didn't call a council of his generals, he didn't proceed to increase his armament, he didn't decide to surrender. He went to God's house. He took that letter and just spread it before the Lord and asked God to save Judah from these fierce enemies. And what happened? That night God sent His angel down and 185,000 Assyrians were slain.

Now modern man would say, "That couldn't have happened. The atomic bombs which fell on Hiroshima and Nagasaki did not kill that many." But God is more powerful than all the power man could ever develop and God did slay the Assyrians and save His people. Do you think anything is too hard for God? Then you need to reverse your thinking. You need to see that God is absolutely sovereign and there is nothing impossible with Him.

But in this message let us turn away from physical feats and think about what God can do in the spiritual realm. Our text contains only three words, "He is able."

### I. He Is Able to Save Unto the Uttermost

It matters not how deep man goes in his sin, God can save him. Paul said, "Christ came to save sinners, of whom I am chief." Look at Paul when he still bore the name of Saul. He was a bigoted Pharisee, he thought he was about the best man God had in the world. Yet he hated Christ and Christians. He thought he was doing God a great service when he sought out these Christians and put them to death. Can God do anything with such a man? Yes, one day on the Damascus Road He halted this man, convicted him of his sin and transformed him completely. The chief of sinners became the chief of saints.

"He saves them to the uttermost," says the writer of Hebrews. That means not only that God saves from the uttermost depths of sin, but He saves unto entire completeness. When a man comes to God through faith in the Lord Jesus Christ he is completely saved. Saved from the past, saved in the present, saved for the future. "The blood of Jesus Christ his Son cleanseth us from all sin" (1 John 1:7).

I well remember the first revival I ever conducted. The little church in Atlanta had called me, young and inexperienced and ignorant as I was, to be their pastor. I had been there just a few weeks when the people said, "We need a revival in our church." So we began to make preparations for the meeting. In our pre-revival cottage prayer meetings the Spirit of God manifested Himself in great power. The people poured out their hearts to God, praying for themselves and for others. The meeting began with services every night for two weeks. God blessed with conversions at every service. I have learned many things since then but in that meeting I learned what God could do, even though His messenger was weak in so many ways.

Well, one of the families in the church had a wayward, sinful son. He was not in Atlanta, and the family didn't know where he was. Then one night after the service I was invited into this home for some refreshments and fellowship. Before I left we formed a circle in the living room and prayed for the revival. I noticed that the burden of nearly every prayer was for this lost prodigal son. On the day before the meeting closed that boy came home. Something had drawn him back from another state. That something was Someone, even the Holy Spirit. On the last night of the meeting that young fellow came to church. The little building was packed with people and he had to sit in an open window. When the invitation was given at the close of the sermon that prodigal who had run the whole gamut of human sin came down the aisle, weeping his way to the foot of the cross. Later he said, "My heavy burden of sin was lifted when I went forward and gave my heart to Christ."

Jesus not only saves the down-and-out, but also the up-and-out. There are many men in this world who have all the material things the world can give them, yet they are not happy, they have no peace in their hearts. But over the years we have seen many of them turn from the world to Christ, who gave them true joy and real happiness.

Christ performed many miracles while He was on the earth. He gave sight to the blind, a new body to the lame, a new life to the dead. But today He is performing even greater miracles in saving sinners. When I was pastor of the First Baptist Church of El Paso, Texas, a young man was given the title of "Mr. El Paso" because of his marvelous physique. Physically he was almost perfect, but he was lost. The pastor in his neighborhood visited him and invited him to church. He went to church, the Holy Spirit moved upon him and he gave his heart to Jesus. But because of his stand for Christ his father cut him out of his will. This cost him $35,000. His pastor said to him, "Did it cost you $35,000 to be a Christian?" "Yes," replied the young man, "but it would have been cheap at many times that much."

Yes, God is able. He is able to save all who come to Him by faith in Christ. And that's the only way to get to God. Not by works, not by baptism, not by church membership, but through "repentance toward God and faith toward our Lord Jesus Christ" (Acts 20:21).

## II. God Is Able to Transform Lives

Some people think salvation is intended only to save from hell. No, as we come to Christ, not only does He save our souls, He changes our lives. If your life hasn't been changed, maybe it's because you were not really and truly saved in the first place. When you come to Christ, as the old preachers used to say, "the things you once loved you now hate and the things you once hated you now love."

The truly converted man has an altogether changed attitude about everything. Before he was saved he saw no harm in many worldly practices. After he was saved he said, "I can't do that now, I am a child of God."

In some of our song books you will find hymns written by William S. Jacoby. Let me tell you his story. He served his country during the Civil War. After the war he secured a position on the Philadelphia police force, but he was so evil he was soon discharged. He joined the regular army and went out west to fight in the Indian Wars. He was so obstreperous that much of his time was spent in the guardhouse. He received a dishonorable discharge and went to

Omaha. He got in trouble there and was given 24 hours to leave town. He went to another town but was just as lawless as ever. Then one night he and another man attended a revival being conducted by Dr. R. A. Torrey. The Holy Spirit brought him under deep conviction. Realizing his need of help he went forward and knelt at the altar, confessing his sins and trusting Christ as his Saviour. He was 42 years old at the time. His life was completely changed. He became a true Christian and served the Lord as long as he lived.

Yes, God is able to turn all that is vile and sinful into all that is good and noble.

### III. God Is Able to Keep Us From Falling

*Jude 24* says, "Now unto him who is able to keep you from falling, and to present you faultless before the presence of his glory with exceeding joy."

Here is a blessed truth — God is not only able to save, but He keeps forever those whom He does save. Many people cannot see that, they believe that God can save you one day and that Satan can snatch you out of His hands the next day. That is saying that Satan is mightier than God and that can never be true.

Listen to *John 10:28-29* — "And I give unto them eternal life; and they shall never perish, neither shall any man pluck them out of my hand. My Father, which gave them me, is greater than all; and no man is able to pluck them out of my Father's hand." Now Jesus is here saying He gives eternal life and we know that is true. Then He says no man nor power can pluck a Christian out of His hand or the Father's hand.

If a person is once joined to Christ in salvation that person and Christ will never be separated. A man who is joined to a woman may be separated by death or divorce. But the man who is joined to Christ is joined to Him forever.

*Romans 8:38-39* — "For I am persuaded, that neither death, nor life, nor angels, nor principalities, nor powers, nor things present, nor things to come, nor height, nor depth, nor any other creature, shall be able to separate us from the love of God, which is in Christ Jesus, our Lord."

A religion which says you can be saved today and lost tomorrow brings no joy and no peace. So we see from God's Word and from human logic that one who has been really saved by the grace of God may never be lost. God has gone to great lengths to make you His child and He is not going to let the devil take you away from Him.

## IV. God Is Able to Fill the Heart With Joy

*1 Peter 1:8* — "Whom having not seen, ye love; in whom, though now ye see him not, yet believing, ye rejoice with joy unspeakable and full of glory."

Who wrote these words? Peter, the man who was once so sad and broken over his denial of Christ that he wept bitterly through the night. But now his joy was unspeakable.

I have heard people say, "Too much religion drives people crazy." That may be true of some false religion, but a sincere faith in the Lord Jesus Christ doesn't hurt anyone. In fact, the coming of Jesus into the heart has saved many persons from insanity.

If you are not a happy Christian it may be because you don't have the right relationship to God. There may be some secret sin standing between you and Him. No life is without its troubles and hardships, but even when these things overwhelm the Christian he can be happy with Christ in his heart.

## V. God Is Able to Use You in His Service

"Oh," you say, "I have no talent, I can't do anything for the Lord." But listen to the words of the great apostle in *1 Corinthians 1:27-29*, "But God hath chosen the foolish things of the world to confound the wise; and God hath chosen the weak things of the world to confound the things which are mighty; and base things of the world, and things which are despised, hath God chosen, yea, and things which are not, to bring to nought the things that are; that no flesh should glory in his presence."

Who are the people who serve in the church and keep the Lord's work going? Not the great, the brilliant, the prominent people, but the faithful people. God can use even the least of us if we put ourselves in His hands.

### VI. God Is Able to Keep His Promises

God called Abraham and told him that from his loins there would come a great nation and from that nation would come the world's Messiah and Saviour. But Abraham was 100 years old and his wife, Sarah, was 90 years old. How could they have a child? But God made His promise and Abraham believed it, although Sarah laughed at it. To her the idea was ridiculous. But God performed a miracle and Isaac was born. God kept His promise.

God's Book is full of the promises of God and God is able to keep every one of them. A dear old lady put the two letters, "T and P," by many of the promises in the Bible. When she was asked what she meant by using these letters alongside these promises she replied, "I meant that they had been tried and proved."

### VII. God Is Able to Raise Us From the Dead

*John 6:39-40* — "And this is the Father's will which hath sent me, that of all which he hath given me I should lose nothing, but should raise it up again at the last day. And this is the will of him that sent me, that every one which seeth the Son, and believeth on him, may have everlasting life; and I will raise him up at the last day."

Life does not end at the grave. The work of Christ in us

does not end at death. The best part begins then. That is why Billy Graham says he looks forward to death. What is the procedure? If the Lord tarries each of us will die, our bodies will be buried, but our spirits will go up to be with Him. Then when He comes in the air our bodies will be raised, He will bring our spirits with Him, our bodies and spirits will be joined and we shall be forever with the Lord. That is the consummation of our salvation.

Today God stands at the door of your heart and says, "I am able to save you unto the uttermost if you come to Christ. I am able to transform your life and keep you from falling. I am able to fill your heart with joy and use you in My service. I am able to keep My promises. I am able to raise you up at the last day and give you eternal bliss." All this and more He can and will do for you if you will put your whole trust in Him.

Years ago in New York City a young woman of twenty-five was living in sin. Her mother had sold her into prostitution when she was a teenage girl. She knew no other life but this life of misery and unhappiness. One night she came out of a bar, leaned against a lamp-post and groaned in her misery. It happened that a fine Christian man who was called "Uncle Charlie" by those who knew him, came along at this time. He talked to the young woman about a great Saviour and sent her to a place where she would be sheltered and cared for. Before long he had led her to a sincere acceptance of Christ.

Her life was transformed, her sin was blotted out. She became a woman of beautiful character and often stood up in church, told the people what Christ had done for her and pled with them to trust Him as Saviour and Lord. But her past life took its toll upon her body and she didn't live long. On the last night of her life the man who had won her to Christ visited her and found the smile of heaven upon her face. "Uncle Charlie," she said, "in a little while I will see

Jesus who loved me and died for me and saved me." And before long she had gone into the presence of the King.

If God is able to take a poor broken creature like that and transform her and take her to His home above, He can do the same thing for you. Won't you take Him as your Saviour and Lord?

# 8.

# Sins of Bible Saints

## (Part One)

*1 John 1:1-10*

One fact stands out clearly about people who have been saved, people who have been born again, people who are the children of God, people who are on the way to heaven. This fact is that they do sin from time to time. There is no such thing as sinless perfection among the sons of men. Jesus Christ is the only Man who ever walked through this world without sin. And when one glorious day He takes us up to be with Him, we shall be like Him and there will be no more sin in us. But as long as we are human, as long as we retain our old carnal nature, as long as we live in a world of temptation, we are going to sin in some way.

(1) *That sin may be in the thought life.* It may be a sinful imagination that no one knows about but God and ourselves. Yet that sin often leads to outward sin. "As a man thinketh in his heart so is he."

(2) *That sin may be outward and open.* It is a pity that so many Christians sin in such a way as to bring reproach upon the cause of Christ, thus becoming a stumbling block to the unsaved.

(3) *That sin may be a secret sin.* No one else may know about this sin but when you kneel to pray there is that sin standing between you and God.

(4) *That sin may be a sin of the tongue.* Some Christians intersperse their speech with words and phrases and jokes which they should not indulge in.

(5) *That sin may be the sin of the disposition.* You may have the wrong feeling or attitude toward someone else. This is just as surely a sin as adultery or drunkenness or theft. The Christian who commits this sin stands guilty before a God of love and mercy.

(6) *That sin may be failure upon your part in the matter of your Christian responsibility.* "To him that knoweth to do good, and doeth it not, to him it is sin" (James 4:17).

(7) *That sin may simply be an indifference to the things of God.* I am trying to say that Christians, however devoted they may be, are not perfect. They often commit sins of one kind or the other. So let us look, in this message, at two men of the Bible who undoubtedly belonged to God, but who were guilty of sin.

## I. First, We Look at Moses

Surely Moses was a saved man, a man of God, the greatest man in the Old Testament. He was reared by a godly mother, then the time came for him to make a choice. He could be the rich ruler of Egypt or a man who gave his life to the liberation of God's children from Egyptian bondage. What did he do? He turned his back upon position and wealth and the pleasures of sin and chose to suffer affliction with the people of God. We are told in the book of Hebrews that Moses felt that Christ meant more to him than all the riches of Egypt. Yes, he was God's man. God laid His hand on him and used him to lead nearly three million people out of Egypt and right to the edge of the Promised Land.

For forty years Moses looked forward to going into Canaan with the Israelites. He endured all kinds of trouble with these ex-slaves, but always ahead of him was this glorious goal. Why, then, did he die just outside of the land? It was because of his sin. Certainly there were other sins in his life, but let us think now of just this one sin.

Often Moses became angry with the people he was leading. It is never a good thing for a leader to become angry with his people for then he becomes a poor leader. But for forty years these people had been as cantankerous as only people could be. They blamed Moses for everything that went wrong. Suddenly he lost his temper.

Here is what happened. The people needed water, so God told Moses to hold his rod up before the people, the rod which represented the authority of God. Then he was to speak to the rock and the water would gush out. But when Moses stood before the people he forgot about God. In anger he shouted, "Must we bring water out of this rock for you, you rebels?" Then Moses struck the rock instead of speaking to it as God had commanded. Water did come out of the rock for God knew the need of the people and provided for them.

Later God took Moses aside and said to him, "You didn't glorify Me at the rock. You took all the credit to yourself. You directly disobeyed Me, so you will not be allowed to go into the Land of Promise." When Moses cooled off he thought of what he had lost. All his life he had dreamed of going into God's country with God's people. Now, because of his hot temper, all his dreams were shattered.

Do I hear someone saying, "I wouldn't give a cent for a person who doesn't have some temper, some fire"? Yes, but when that fire begins to burn someone else, you are guilty of sin.

Anger weakens a man and causes him to play into the hands of his enemy. When Sinbad and his sailors landed on a tropical island they saw high up in the trees some coconuts which could quench their thirst and satisfy their hunger. The coconuts were too high for them to reach, but a group of chattering monkeys were in the trees. So the men began to throw rocks at the monkeys. The monkeys became so angry they began to seize the coconuts and throw them down. This, of course, was just what the men wanted. So when we permit someone to make us angry we become subservient to them.

The pity about anger and a hot temper is that we often use them on the ones we love the most. A man may be very sweet and even-tempered at the office but at home he often engages in bursts of temper which ruin the whole atmosphere of the home and upsets his entire family. . . . And a woman who is so nice at a Sunday school party or at the P.T.A. often goes home and explodes all over her family.

An aged man went to a doctor for a check-up. The doctor said, "You are the most robust man for your age that I ever saw. What is the secret of your strength and good health?" The man replied, "I have been compelled to live an out-door life. When my wife and I married we agreed that when I lost my temper she was to keep quiet and when she lost her temper I was to go out of doors. My wife lost her temper so often I've spent most of my time out in the fresh air. That is the reason for my good health."

Moses was a good man, a great man, a godly man, but when he lost his temper he lost infinitely more, he lost the Promised Land. And I'm sure many Christians lose many wonderful blessings because of a bad temper.

Well, what is the remedy for a hot temper? Christ is the remedy for every sin. Take your bad temper to Him in prayer. Ask Him to help you to have self-control. He'll do it. When you feel a tantrum coming on, when your temper flares up, when you feel the blood rushing to your head, ask the Lord to help you get hold of yourself. Keep up this practice and you'll whip that sin of a hot temper.

## II. Next, We Look at Samson

In Hebrews 11 God puts Samson in the Hall of Faith, so we believe he was a man of God. Of course we always think of him first as a man of tremendous strength. God made him just that. He could whip all the modern heavyweights with one hand tied behind his back. He performed many deeds of great strength. He killed a lion single-handedly, he slew a thousand Philistines with the jawbone of an ass, he carried off the heavy gates of Gaza.

There was only one thing that stopped Samson and that was sin. He was no match for it, sin ruined him. We see him going down to Sorek to see a woman named Delilah. He was infatuated with her and he sinned greatly with her. He betrayed his high trust and followed Satan and forgot God. The Philistine lords went to Delilah one day and said, "This man Samson is an enemy of our country. If you will entice him and get him to tell you the secret of his great strength each of us will give you eleven hundred pieces of silver." The amount would total $3,375.00 which would have seemed like a fortune in that day.

You know the story. The next time Samson came to see Delilah she kept teasing him and vexing him until he finally gave in and told her that his strength lay in his long hair. So Delilah made Samson fall asleep, then called for the lords to come in and cut off his hair. After that she awakened him with the cry, "Wake up, Samson, the Philistines are here." But Samson remembered his great strength which God had given him and and he ran out to overcome the Philistines. Alas, he was helpless, he could do nothing, his strength was gone. Now we read this sad commentary, "And he knew not that the Lord was departed from him" (Judg. 16:20). He was completely unconscious of the fearful loss he had sustained.

Today we see many illustrations of the same thing. Men

and women who have been living for Christ and who have been active in the church begin to flirt with the world. They go out and taste the things of Satan. They neglect their prayer life, they leave off their simple Christian duties, they give up some of their Christian convictions. Soon their spiritual power is gone and they hardly realize it.

Now Samson's strength lay not primarily in his hair, but in the fact that God was with him. His long hair was a part of his vow as a Nazarite. When that vow was broken God's strength left him. God promises us spiritual strength but never when we are disobedient to Him.

One day one of my church members came to me and said, "Pastor, I am going to take a Sunday job, I need the financial help. While I will not be able to come to church I am going to read my Bible and pray and I know the Lord will bring me through." I tried to tell him he couldn't expect the Lord to bless him if he didn't honor God and God's day. And it turned out just that way. His promises of blessing are not to those who break His commandments and neglect His service.

Now back to Samson. Where did his downfall begin? It began when he went after this sinful woman. And many a young man has met his downfall in the same way. Listen to the wise words in *Proverbs 7:21-27*, "With her much fair speech she caused him to yield, with the flattering of her lips, she forced him. He goeth after her straightway, as an ox goeth to the slaughter, or as a fool to the correction of the stocks; till a dart strike through his liver; as a bird hasteth to the snare; and knoweth not that it is for his life. Hearken unto me therefore, O ye children, and attend to the words of my mouth. Let not thine heart decline to her ways, go not astray in her paths. For she hath cast down many wounded, yea, many strong men have been slain by her. Her house is the way to hell, going down to the chambers of death."

When the Philistines saw how helpless Samson was, they took him captive with ease. Like us, without God Samson was nothing. The first thing they did to him was to put out his eyes with a red-hot iron. You can imagine how painful that was. His eyes had looked upon sin, now he loses them. Then they bound him with chains of brass. His feet had walked the ways of sin, now they are bound. Then they placed him in a prison cell. The free man who had gone where he pleased is now a slave. Then they forced him to grind at the mill. The mighty man had fallen to the lowest depths.

As you look upon that poor blind man going around and around at the mill you see what sin can do for a man. Sin blinds, sin binds, sin grinds.

Young man, young woman, let me ask you a question. Do you think you can get away with sin? Samson didn't. Do you think you are stronger than Samson? We are living in a loose age, the bars are let down on every side, morals are lower than ever. But hear the words of the Lord, "The wages of sin is death. Whatsoever a man soweth that shall he also reap." It was true 100 years ago, it was true 1000 years ago, and it is true today.

How can a Christian avoid the sin that ruined Samson? He can turn to Christ who is our only hope in time of temptation.

> Take the Name of Jesus with you,
> As a shield from every snare,
> When temptations round you gather,
> Breathe that holy Name in prayer.

In the Bible we read of another man who had the same temptation as Samson. His name was Joseph. His temptation was greater for if he had yielded to it he would have gained high position and great power. But instead he said, "This thing is wrong in God's sight, I can't do it." His decision sent him to prison, but he knew he had done the right thing. So instead of ending up as Samson did, God elevated him to the highest position in Egypt.

A great Scotch preacher had lost his mother when he was a small boy. But when she was on her deathbed he made some sort of covenant with her which he promised to keep until he met her in heaven. No one ever knew what that covenant was but he often said the secret treaty he made with his mother kept him safe when he was assailed by temptations.

So let me urge you to make a covenant with Jesus. Let it be a covenant of dedication to Him and a holy vow to keep yourself unspotted from the world. You may not always be able to keep this vow perfectly, just as a bath does not always keep you clean, but you'll be a better Christian for having made this covenant.

And what should a Christian do when sin has tripped him up? He should hasten to the mercy seat, get down on his knees and ask God to forgive him. God provides forgiveness for the Christian who sins. He says that if we sin we have an advocate with the Father, even Jesus Christ the righteous. I am glad we have Him to represent us at the throne of God. He also says that if we confess our sin He is faithful and just to forgive our sin and to cleanse us from all unrighteousness.

I am sure that every one of us has some sins in our lives today. Of course, there are some people who are so good-goody and self-righteous they can't see their own sins. I am urging you to join me in bowing your head in confession before God today, asking for God's forgiveness. But remember that our confession has no effect unless we forsake our sin.

Are you guilty of some sin of commission? Then bring it out before God and tear it out of your heart. Are you guilty of some sin of omission, are you neglecting your simple

Christian responsibilities? Then tell God that from now on you are going to be more faithful. Are you guilty of the sin of the disposition? Then tell God that from now on you're going to love those whom you have been hating.

In the book, *Quo Vadis,* there is a man by the name of Chilo. After a very wicked life he was saved under the preaching of the Apostle Paul. At this time Nero was putting thousands of Christians to death. Some of his victims were covered with pitch, fastened to pillars along the avenues or in the gardens and set on fire for the amusement of Nero.

So Chilo was taken out by his torturers, bound with ropes, covered with pitch and made ready for the fire. But all the time they were torturing him, he was kissing their hands in love and forgiveness and speaking sweetly to them.

Have you sinned? Then in like manner Jesus is ready to give you His kiss of love and forgiveness, for He says, "Come now, and let us reason together, saith the Lord: though your sins be as scarlet, they shall be as white as snow; though they be red like crimson, they shall be as wool" (Isa. 1:18).

# 9.

# Sins of Bible Saints
## (Part Two)

### *2 Peter 2:7-9*

In my previous sermon on this subject, I spoke of the sins of two Old Testament characters, Moses the great leader and lawgiver and Samson the man of great strength and flagrant sin. In this sermon let us think about the sins of three other men of God, Lot, David and Simon Peter.

As we speak of the "sins of the saints" we need to define the word "saint" as it is used in the Bible. According to the Roman church a saint is one who has led a good life and piled up many good deeds, then years after his death the church hierarchy elects him as a "saint." But this is not the Bible definition of a saint. According to the New Testament a saint is anyone who has trusted Christ as his Saviour and been born again. Often Paul refers to his fellow Christians as saints. In the Old Testament a saint was one who had trusted God and who was looking forward in faith to the coming of the Messiah, Christ.

If a saint had to be a perfect person there would never be a saint on earth or in heaven, for even as we look at the best men in the Bible we see that even they have sinned at some time. So let us look at these three men, men who belonged to God but who were human beings after all and who were subject to sin.

## I.  FIRST, WE THINK OF LOT

According to the New Testament Lot was a saved man. God called him a "just man," a "righteous man," a "godly man" (2 Peter 2:7-9). Now Lot was an example of a worldly Christian. He spent years under the influence of Abraham, his godly uncle. But when the time came for him to make a choice between Godliness and worldliness he made his choice for the latter. He could have remained as a cattleman on the ranch or he could have gone into business in the wicked city of Sodom. He was attracted by the bright lights and gay life of the city. Like so many Christians today he was lured by the world. So we see him going into Sodom and living there. He made the wrong choice.

Lot soon became a backslider. He called the wicked men of Sodom his "brethren." He drank their cocktails with them, he played their cards with them. He soon became a very popular man and was elected as one of the city officials. But what about his faith in God? There was a lapse in that faith, he didn't live for God before his family or his associates. He dwelt in a wicked worldly city and entered into its wickedness and its worldliness.

Well, the time came when God decided that Sodom would have to be destroyed because of its wickedness. In His mercy He sent some angels down to warn Lot to get out of Sodom before its destruction. Suddenly Lot saw his danger and prepared to leave the city. Of course, he didn't want his family to perish so he rushed to the homes of his married daughters to warn them. But they laughed at him as he talked about God and angels and judgment. They had lost all confidence in his religion. A Christian can't sink down in sin and expect to lift anyone up. If you lift anyone up you must be on a higher level than he is.

So what happened to Lot and his family? He and his wife and his unmarried daughters got out of Sodom safely but his married daughters and their families perished beneath the hail and brimstone. Then even as they fled from the city Lot's wife looked back upon the city and the life she lived there and was turned into a pillar of salt. Lot was able to get her out of Sodom, but he couldn't get Sodom out of her. He was able also to get his unmarried daughters out of Sodom, but even they sank down into the lewdest kind of sin.

A Christian can't run with the world and expect the Lord to bless him. I have seen many of them turn their backs upon God and the church and go out to serve the world. Then when trouble came to them they cried out, "Why did God let this happen to me?" *1 John 2:15* says, "Love not the world, neither the things that are in the world. If any man love the world, the love of the Father is not in him." Now, what is worldliness? It is anything that stands between you and God and keeps you from being the Christian you ought to be.

Many of our people are engaged in things not harmful in themselves, but these things do keep them from giving their best to Christ and His church, so I say that these things are not right for a Christian. Some Christians feel they must go along with the world to gain business advantage or social prestige, so they go to the places where sinners go and do the things worldlings do. Soon they look and act so much like the world they lose their Christian influence and power.

For a Christian to have any influence for God and for good he must be a different person from the worldlings around him. One of our young peoples' organizations once had the motto, "Dare to be different." A Christian should live in such a way as to cause those outside of Christ to say, "He is different, He has something I do not have, it makes him a finer person. I would like to have what he has."

Wordsworth said, "The world is too much with us." Yes,

day in and day out the world presses in upon us, using every device to lure us away from God. That is one reason God created a day of worship for us, when we can come and wash our souls clean and get new strength for the battles of everyday life and our conflicts with Satan. That is also the reason Christ instituted the church. He wants it to be the voice that calls us from a world of care and unto the Father's presence.

Yes, Lot was like so many modern-day Christians. He had his name in God's book, he was saved. But he thought more of the things of the world than of the things of God, he thought more of his pleasures than of his religion, he thought more of his life than of the life to come. So Lot lost out, though he was saved, he lost his family, he lost his influence, he lost his peace of mind. His soul was saved, but his life was lost.

Oh, Christian, it is not enough just to be saved. Don't be content just to get your name on a church roll. Put the world behind you, the cross before you and give your best to Christ.

## II. NEXT WE LOOK AT DAVID

There is no doubt but that David was a man of God. God called him "a man after my own heart." God anointed him and blessed him and used him in a wonderful way. God gave him power to reign as Israel's great king. David wrote the finest tributes to God ever penned. But, and that "but" applies to every man, David sinned greatly.

The circumstances of David's sin are well known to every Bible student. One day he was idling on the housetop simply doing nothing. "An idle brain is the devil's workshop." So in this moment David was sorely tempted. He looked over next door and saw a beautiful woman at her bath. Tempted by the flesh he coveted this woman for himself. So, being the king and having the power to do as he pleased, he had her brought over to his palace where he sinned with her greatly. But this was not the extent of his sin. Since he wanted Bathsheba for himself, he planned to get rid of her husband. So he sent the husband into the front line of battle where he knew he would be killed. Then when he learned of the husband's death he took Bathsheba for his wife.

Oh, David, man of God, how grievously you sinned, how many of God's commandments you broke, how many people you hurt! The Bible says, "Thou shalt have no other gods before me," but you put the god of lust before the God of heaven. The Bible says, "Thou shalt not covet," but you coveted your neighbor's wife. The Bible says, "Thou shalt not commit adultery," but you were guilty of this sin. The Bible says, "Thou shalt not kill," but you had a man killed so you could get his wife for yourself.

Is this the man after God's own heart? Is this the man who wrote, "The Lord is my shepherd"? Is this the man who said, "God is my refuge and my strength"? Yes, this is the man, God's man. The Bible says, "Let him that thinketh he standeth, take heed lest he fall." What is the lesson here? No matter how good you have been in the past, no matter how active you have been for God, every Christian is subject to temptation and sin.

Well, David didn't immediately confess his sin. He waited a year. Did he go to church? On one occasion he said, "I was glad when they said unto me, 'Let us go into the house of the Lord.'" He might have gone to the Lord's house during that time, but surely he found no joy in it for always that sin loomed up before him when he tried to worship. Did he pray during that time? We often hear him saying, "I cried unto the Lord and He heard me." But if he prayed at all there was that sin always standing between him and God, for David also said, "If I regard iniquity in my heart the Lord will not hear me."

About a year later the prophet Nathan visited David.

I believe David was so miserable and so far from God he was glad to see the preacher and to listen to him. So Nathan told David a little story of the injustice shown by a rich man, a story that aroused David to red-hot anger. In fact David said, "That man ought to be killed." Then the preacher pointed his finger at David and said, "Thou art the man." And poor old David broke down and cried out, "I have sinned." And the preacher replied, "The Lord also hath put away thy sin." How David must have rejoiced, how relieved he must have been, how his heart must have sung with joy!

If you as a Christian can sin and feel comfortable about it, there's something wrong with you. But if you sin and it bothers you, if it burdens your conscience, if it breaks your fellowship with God, then you need to come confessing as David did. Surely then the Lord will forgive your sin. In David's prayer of confession as recorded in Psalm 51 he cries out, "Restore unto me the joy of thy salvation." He had not lost his salvation but he had certainly lost the joy of it. If you are a real Christian, you'll not be lost and sent to hell because of some sin, but you'll lose the joy and the peace of your salvation. Oh, the misery of a joyless Christian life.

Here is a man who kills another man. He may be very sorry for his act of violence, the state may pardon him, but that will not bring the dead man back to life again. So David was forgiven but he still had to suffer the consequences of his sin. First, the baby born to that tragic union died. Then his daughter Tamar was raped by her half-brother, Ammon. Then David's beloved favorite son, Absalom, killed Ammon. Then, tragedy of tragedies, Absalom himself tried to steal his father's throne and was killed by Joab. In his deep sorrow we now hear David sobbing out, "O my son Absalom, my son, my son Absalom! Would God I had died for thee, O Absalom, my son, my son." And poor old David went down to the grave with a broken heart, brought on by his own sin.

Oh, Christian, don't think you can sin and get away with it. Sin pays off in the bitterest coin. And don't think God is blind to sin. "Be sure your sin will find you out" (Num. 32:23).

### III. LASTLY WE LOOK AT SIMON PETER

Certainly Peter was a Christian. He was gloriously saved when his brother Andrew brought him to Christ. Jesus called him to be a disciple and used him mightily as a preacher. Peter finally died for the sake of his Saviour. He walked three and a half years by the side of the Greatest Soul who ever touched the world, he heard the greatest sermons ever preached, he felt the impact of the sweetest spirit who ever lived. He was Christ's chief and greatest disciple. But, and there's that "but" again, he also sinned greatly because his sin was against love.

One day Jesus said to His disciples, "I am going up to Jerusalem where wicked men will arrest me and kill me." Then big old lovable, impulsive Peter blurted out, "Oh no, Master, they won't do that. They'll have to kill me before they touch you." But Jesus could look down into men's hearts and he recognized Peter's weakness. "Peter," Jesus said, "before the cock crows thou shalt deny me three times." But again Peter protested he would die before he would allow anyone to harm his Lord.

Later that night Jesus took His disciples into the Garden of Gethsemane to pray. As they came forth from the place of prayer cruel hands seized Jesus and arrested Him. He was hurried by his captors to a midnight trial. Where is Peter now? He said he would defend Jesus to the death. Where is he? Is he by Jesus' side, is he fighting in His behalf? No, no, he is out yonder by the enemies' fire, warming himself against the cold night air. Suddenly a little serving maid came up and said to him, "Aren't you a friend of Jesus? Weren't you with Him?" And Peter replied, "Jesus? Jesus who? I don't know what you are talking about." Then another maid said to the group, "I saw this fellow with Jesus of Nazareth." And Peter said, "I don't know the man." Then someone said to him, "You surely are one of His followers, your speech betrays you." Peter was so angry by this time that he began to curse, saying, "I know not the man."

Is this Simon Peter who is cursing and lying about his relationship to Christ? Is this the man who declared that Jesus was "the Christ, the Son of the Living God?" Is this the man who swore he would die for Jesus? Yes, this is the man, the Christian, the Chief Apostle, but he is also the man who sinned greatly against the One who loved him more than anyone on earth loved him.

Now we witness a scene filled with deepest pathos. Just as soon as Peter denied Jesus he heard a cock crowing and he remembered the words of Jesus. Then as Jesus was led out of the council chamber He looked into the eyes of Peter. It was not a look of rebuke, it was a look of love and compassion and mercy and forgiveness. That look broke Peter's heart and he went outside, leaned against the wall and wept like a baby.

Is that the end of the story? No, Christ went on to Calvary to die for Peter and you and me. Then He came back and let Peter know he had been forgiven and then He gave Peter a new commission. And Peter, full of penitence and his heart overflowing with love for his compassionate Saviour, went out and gave his life away in the service of Christ, dying as a martyr.

Dear Christian friend, have you denied Jesus? You will say, "No, preacher, if anyone asks me if I know the Saviour I will gladly tell them I know and love Him." Ah, but there are other ways to deny Him. You deny Him when you fail to stand up for what He stands for. You deny Him when you put something else before Him and His church. When you hold a glass of whiskey in your hands you are denying Him. When you show complete indifference to Him and His cause you are denying Him. When you spend all He gives you on yourself and give nothing to Him, you are denying Him. You are saying other things are more important than Christ. When you neglect your Christian responsibilities you are denying Him. When your life does not reflect His life you are denying Him.

Listen, Christian, don't you hear the cock crowing in your soul? Can't you see how you have denied Christ? He's looking at you, He's loving you, He's dying for you. Why do you go on denying Him? Why don't you say right now, "From now on I'll never deny Him again. I am going to clean up my life and live for Him as a Christian should!"

An old man lay dying in one of our hospitals. In the last days he lost his eyesight. The days were long and tiresome for him except when his granddaughter would come and read to him. One day she was reading the first chapter of First John when he stopped her and said, "Wait, what was that you just read?" And again she read the words, "The blood of Jesus Christ His Son cleanseth us from all sin." "Does it really say that?" the old man asked. "Yes," she replied and read it again.

Then he said, "Honey, put my fingers right on the words where it says 'the blood.'" And the granddaughter placed the gnarled old fingers on those very words. Then his lips silently moved as he repeated the words and as God touched his soul. In a few minutes he breathed his last breath, but before that moment he said, "You can say that I died believing that the blood of Jesus Christ has cleansed me from all sin."

Dear friend, that cleansing is for you, too. Come to Him and let Him wash you as white as snow.

# 10.

# The Friend Everybody Needs

Acts 26:24-29

In our text we see the Apostle Paul standing before King Agrippa. With fierce earnestness he tells the king about his conversion, about his meeting Christ on the Damascus Road. The king, being greatly moved, said, "Almost thou persuadest me to be a Christian." And the compassionate preacher cried out, "I would to God that you were a Christian."

What did the king need most? Not money, not power, not culture. He needed Christ. Oh, how much Christ could have done for King Agrippa! And what a great power he could have been for Christ. Can you imagine what mighty influence our presidents and rulers could be today if they were devoted followers of Jesus Christ?

Here is a mother in the home. She has the children to be reared in the right way, the home to be cared for, the meals to be prepared. But what does she need most? She needs a Saviour. Here is a father with many business cares besetting him. But what does he need most? He needs a Saviour. Here is a criminal facing a prison sentence. But what does he need most? He needs a Saviour. Here is a man in darkest Africa bowing down before an idol of wood or stone. What does he need most? He needs a Saviour. What does the richest man in the world need? He needs

Christ, the only Saviour. What does the poorest man in the world need? He needs a Saviour. And there is only One under heaven who can save him and His Name is Jesus.

I am glad He is my Friend, I am glad He saved me, I am glad He called me to preach. I thank God that He has been with me in a ministry that covers half a century. He is my Friend in joy, my Friend in sorrow, my Friend in sickness and my Friend in health, my Friend now and my Friend forever.

Why does everyone need Jesus? For three reasons. We need Him because of the past, we need Him because of the present, we need Him because of the future.

### I.  We Need Jesus Because of the Past

1. *In the past we have sinned.* We have sinned many times and in many ways. We need to do something about those sins. A boy may fly a kite and when he pleases he may pull it in. But we can't do that with our sinful words and deeds and thoughts. Sometimes a man will commit a sin and spend the rest of his life trying to cover it up. But there is only one covering for sin. The old song tells us what it is.

> There is a fountain filled with blood,
> Drawn from Immanuel's veins,
> And sinners plunged beneath that flood,
> Lose all their guilty stains.

We are told the white ants of Africa are very destructive. A man sits down at night in his favorite chair. The next morning he sits in that chair and it collapses. During the night the white ants have crawled up the center posts of the chair. No one sees them but they eat away the heart of the wood. It is the same way with sin. Sin comes into a man's life, the world doesn't see it, but it eats his life away.

A girl who had been reared in poverty was brought to a Rescue Home in New York. As she grew up she had gone down into the depths of sin and depravity. The first night she was in the home the matron who made the rounds found the girl's bed empty and the girl sleeping under the bed. She asked the girl why she was not in the bed. The girl pointed to the clean sheets and said, "I could never get in that bed. I have never seen anything so clean."

In like manner sin stamps us as guilty and unclean. Then we look at God's holiness and realize we don't deserve His notice. But God is so gracious and merciful He takes our sin away and gives us His righteousness.

Our yesterdays have been filled with sin, the record is a black one. But Jesus says, "Come unto Me and I will remove your sin as far as the east is from the west. I'll cast your sin into the deepest sea, I'll put it behind my back and remember it no more forever." Yes, every man needs a Friend like that.

2. *In the past there are God's blessings.* Ezekiel said, "Thy mercies are new every morning." There are 365 mornings in every year with an extra morning thrown in every four years and every one of the mornings is filled with the blessings of God. Because of these blessings and out of a heart of gratitude we ought to love and follow Jesus.

The old song tells us to "count your blessings, name them one by one." But who can ever count that high? You begin to count and just give up. Your heart fills with gratitude, your eyes fill with tears, and you say, "God has been so good to me, I surely ought to be a Christian."

3. *In the past there are memories.* You remember your mother as she prayed for you, you remember your father as he gave you good advice, you remember your Thanksgiving and Christmas days with your loved ones. They are gone now and your eyes are wet as you think of them. You want

to see them again some day. That means that you need Jesus.

4. *In the past there are resolutions.* One day, in a high moment in God's house, you said, "I'll give myself to Him." One day a great blessing came to you and you said, "I am not worthy of the least of His mercies, I know I ought to live for Him." One day you saw a Christian die, and you said, "I want to be ready when my time comes." But you haven't kept these vows, the days are going by, life is passing. You need Jesus.

So as we look at the past, we see every reason why we should be Christians, we see our need of Jesus, the one true Friend.

## II. We Need Jesus Because of the Present

1. *We need His help in everyday living.* Without Jesus we are lost in a fog. The Christless man is living, but not at his best. He needs Jesus who says, "Come and walk with Me, I know all about life. I have been where you are. I know all the pitfalls and temptations of life, I can help you, I can see you through."

In the Russo-Japanese war a Japanese colonel was captured by the Russians and condemned to be shot to death. They asked him if he had anything to say before he was killed. He took some money out of his pocket and said, "I want you to give this money to the Russian Red Cross." When they asked him why he wanted to give money to his enemies he replied, "Some years ago a missionary came to my country and told me about Jesus Christ. I took Him as my Saviour. Now I want to follow His example by forgiving my enemies as He did when He died upon the cross." Where did he learn this? He learned it from Jesus. We never learn to treat others rightly unless we learn it from Christ and have His spirit in our hearts.

A certain preacher's son was killed in a tragic accident caused by the carelessness of another man. The preacher was broken-hearted but he sat down and wrote a nice letter to the man responsible for his son's death. Where did he learn this? He learned it from Jesus.

When a man seeks revenge, when he says he is going to get even with someone if it's the last thing he does, we know he doesn't have the spirit of Christ. If anyone has wronged you, just leave it with the Lord. He can handle the matter better than you can.

Not only does Jesus teach us right principles, He gives us the power to live up to them. Confucius and Buddha gave their followers some good rules but these leaders are dead. They could not give their followers any power to keep these rules. Only a living Christ can give that power, and He does.

2. *We need a Comforter in the present time.* No one sees more sorrow than a preacher. I remember that in the space of one month as a pastor I was called on to go to a home where a man had committed suicide, to another home where a man had dropped dead, and to another home where a boy accidentally killed his brother. When I was called on to comfort the families all I could do was to point them to Jesus, the One who can comfort a broken heart.

In the Upper Room Jesus said to His disciples, "I am going away, I am going to leave you." Their hearts were broken with sorrow, but Jesus said, "I will not leave you comfortless, I will send you the Comforter." He was referring to the Holy Spirit who abides in the Christian's heart and speaks comfort to him in time of sorrow.

Someone painted a picture of a young woman sitting in deep sorrow. Her husband had just died. Father Time stood by her, looking down upon her in compassion. The title of the picture was, "The Mender of Broken Hearts."

Time is the only comforter the lost man has, but the Christian has a Divine Friend to comfort him.

3. *We need an intercessor in the present time.* My father had several boys but only one girl. Of course that girl was closer to him than any of us boys. So, when I wanted some favor from my father I did not always go to him direct, but asked my sister to intercede for me. And I nearly always got what I wanted when she did this. She was my intercessor. Now Jesus is closer to the Heavenly Father than any of us. He is our intercessor, our advocate who appears before God in our behalf. *Hebrews 7:25* tells us that "He ever liveth to make intercession for us."

So as we look at the present we see that life is too big and too hard for us. We need a friend, we need Jesus every day. And He says, "I'll be with you, I'll go with you to the end."

### III.  We Need Jesus Because of the Future

1. *In the future there is death.* We are reminded of this on every side. Every newspaper tells us of death, every funeral procession reminds us we are headed in the same direction. If the Lord Jesus tarries, death will come to everyone of us.

Look at the leaf on the tree. It will not last. One day when the autumn winds blow it will fall. Look at that beautiful rose in the vase. It will not last, it will soon droop and die. Look at the bloom on the cheek of that youth. It will not last, someday that cheek will lose its bloom and be old and wrinkled. Look at that new house. It will not last, it will rot away with the years. What are all these things telling us? They are telling us that we will not last either, death is coming. In the midst of life there is death, that is why we need Jesus in the future.

They call this world "the land of the living." No, it is the land of the dying. One day, one night, death will creep up on you and me. It is later than you think. Just a few more toils and tears and our journey will be over and we'll meet death. And it is then we'll need a Saviour to take our hands and lead us home.

A French nurse was called upon to nurse a man who was critically ill and near death. She asked the question, "Is he a Christian?" "Yes," came the answer, "but why do you ask?" The nurse replied, "I nursed Voltaire and watched him die. Not for all of Europe would I watch another infidel die."

Thank God, we don't have to die like an infidel. We have a Friend who says, "Fear not, I'll be with you when you come to the dark valley of the shadow of death." Because death is coming we need Jesus.

2. *In the future there is the Judgment.* In the Polish cemeteries the names of the dead are carved on the tombstones just as is the custom in America. They believe that on the last day the good people will be called to life and the bad to eternal doom. But on some of the stones there is no name. Those who are living hope the angels will pass over these graves and leave their occupants sleeping. But that cannot be, no one will escape. God will bring everyone into judgment.

At the judgment some will rejoice as they hear the Lord say, "Here is your reward, enter into the joys of thy Lord." But others will mourn as they realize they are doomed forever, because they have left Jesus out of their lives. Men go to hell for just one reason, their rejection of Jesus Christ.

In 1833 a meteoric shower fell over Scotland in the middle of the night. People thought that this was the end of the world. In a certain home there was a half-witted boy who trusted and loved the Lord Jesus. His mother went to his room and cried out, "Sandy, get up, the judgment day has come." The boy leaped out of bed and shouted, "Glory to God, I'm ready." You can say that only if Christ is your Saviour.

3. *In the future there is eternity.* Death is not all, judgment is not all, there are millions of years beyond these events. Can you count the stars of the heavens? Can you count the grains of sand beside the seven seas? Can you count the drops of water in the ocean? Then you can count the years of eternity. Now the question is — are you going to spend these years with Christ or in an endless hell?

So because of the past and its record, you need Christ. And because of the present and all its demands you need Christ. And because of the future, because of death and judgment and eternity, you need Christ the Saviour. He is the One indispensable Friend, the One you can't do without.

Let me close this sermon with the story of "The Man Who Died for Me." Out on the Pacific coast in the years gone by a man was dying of tuberculosis. He was mean and vile and evil. A good Christian woman came in to minister to his needs and he cursed her. She waited on him for two weeks, preparing his meals and taking care of his house, but he didn't show her the gratitude of a dog. One day the woman brought her little girl with her, and left her just outside of the house while she went inside to serve the man.

The man heard the little girl and said to the woman, "Who is that out there?" When the woman told him it was her little girl he said, "Bring her in the house." When the little girl came and stood by the man's bedside he put his hand upon her head and said, "Once I had a little girl. She loved me as no one else has ever loved me, but she died and since that time I have hated everyone." The woman told him that Christ had taken his little girl to heaven and was keeping her there for him. Then the man said, "Please pray to Him for me and tell Him I want to see my little girl again." Soon the good Christian woman was able to lead the man to Christ.

Some of his friends came in from the mine and he said to them, "Boys, you know how the water runs down into the sluice boxes and takes away the dirt and leaves the gold. Well, that's what the Man did who died for me. He has taken away all my sin and has saved me." Two weeks later the man died, but before he died he said to his friends, "Good-by, boys, I am going to see Mamie and the Man who died for me."

I tell you, a Saviour like that is worth having. He is the best Friend in all the world. Don't you want Him as your Friend?